Breakthrough Management

Breakthrough Management

How to Convert Priority Objectives into Results

GIORGIO MERLI

Translated by Ralph Bullock

JOHN WILEY & SONS

Chichester · New York · Brisbane · Toronto · Singapore

Original Italian edition published under the title of *La Gestione Efficace : Come Trasformare gli Obiettivi in Risultati*

Copyright © 1993 Il Sole 24 Ore Società Editoriale Media Economici, Milano.

English language edition copyright © 1995 by John Wiley & Sons Ltd,
Baffins Lane, Chichester,
West Sussex PO19 1UD, England
National Chichester 01243 779777
International   (+44) 1243 779777

Translated by Ralph Bullock.

Other Wiley Editorial Offices

John Wiley & Sons, Inc., 605 Third Avenue,
New York, NY 10158–0012, USA

Jacaranda Wiley Ltd, 33 Park Road, Milton,
Queensland 4064, Australia

John Wiley & Sons (Canada) Ltd, 22 Worcester Road,
Rexdale, Ontario M9W 1L1, Canada

John Wiley & Sons (SEA) Pte Ltd, 37 Jalan Pemimpin #05–04,
Block B, Union Industrial Building, Singapore 2057

Library of Congress Cataloging-in-Publication Data
Merli, Giorgio.
    [Gestione efficace.   English]
    Breakthrough management : how to convert objectives into results /
Giorgio Merli ; translated by Ralph Bullock.
       p.   cm.
    Includes bibliographical references and index.
    ISBN 0-471-95351-2
    1. Strategic planning.   2. Total quality management.
3. Management by objectives.   I. Title.
HD30.28.M45713   1995
658.4—dc20   94–38626
                                                                        CIP

British Library Cataloguing in Publication Data

A catalogue record for this book is available from the British Library

ISBN 0-471-95351-2

Typeset in 11/13 pt Palatino from translator's disk
by Dorwyn Ltd, Rowlands Castle, Hants
Printed and bound in Great Britain by
Biddles Ltd, Guildford and King's Lynn

To my wife Marina

Contents

Introduction

This book is written for managers who already have, want to have, or will be forced to have major improvement objectives. It is based on the assumption (which makes this theme interesting) that the reader works in a firm in which there is strong pressure for improvement.

This is not a minor assumption, since it is my experience that such a situation is far from common. It is in fact a paradox that while today almost all companies maintain that they need to make major changes, only a small number recognise that they must introduce a way of managing capable of achieving these changes through normal everyday management.

There is a lack of awareness that such changes can be made to happen through an "effective improvement process". Most of the companies still believe that they must and can only be achieved through drastic actions or innovations such as a new technology, a different product or market strategy, a new managing director, etc. There are also many firms which still rely almost exclusively on the behaviour of the market for any possibility of success or turnaround. These firms do not seem to have noticed a situation which today is general and irreversible: market oversupply is now endemic, so that survival and success are strongly dependent on factors of relativity. This means that a business, whatever its market position, will win and be profitable only if it succeeds in achieving better performance than its competitors.

Identifying the level of performance which is "necessary and sufficient" is particularly difficult at times when the improvement trends imposed by the market are particularly strong (a situation which is common today to many market sectors). Indeed, in such cases attention is concentrated more on the levels and trends imposed by the market or by the competitors (for example, reduce prices by 10% or delivery times by 50%) than on the levels which will enable them to reach a position of competitive advantage compared with the others. Therefore it often happens that although they commit themselves to achieving the improvements demanded by the market, businesses risk losing opportunities for extra competitive advantage which are already within their grasp.

For example, a reduction of 60% instead of the 50% in delivery time "imposed" by the market would not call for so much greater an effort, but the result in terms of competitive advantage could be completely different. The market, making comparisons between what suppliers propose, will obviously be very appreciative of the extra 10% offered, while the 50% already offered by all the other competitors will merely meet the new benchmark (the level of performance which all firms must guarantee if they wish to compete).

The other fundamental dimension in this context is time. The same improvement in a result is quite different in terms of value depending on when it is offered to the market. Thus a 50% reduction in delivery time offered before the competition probably means an increase in market share. The same improvement offered after the competition (even 6 months later) is probably only just enough to stabilise a market share which has already shrunk. The efforts made to achieve it are then only the cost of catching up with the competition.

It must therefore be recognised that the competitive advantage of a business depends on its capacity to improve its operating performance, and that the improvement trend and the time that it takes to achieve it constitute the discriminating factor between failure and success. This means that we must recognise the need for an improvement management system which is more "effective" than that of our competitors (where effective means "capability in terms of quantity and speed of result").

This book proposes an approach and a methodology for achieving precisely this goal, the effective management of the improvement priorities of a business. It is an original management model, combining a Japanese approach (Management by Policy), some instruments developed by the Deming prizewinner Ryuji Fukuda (the SEDAC system) and Priority Planning and Management systems developed by Galgano & Associates.

The model has already been chosen by a dozen multinational firms and by many European companies of a wide range of sizes. The successes which they have enjoyed are the main reasons for writing this book. The logic of the management model proposed can also be seen as a further development of the Total Quality approach, which is now increasingly aimed at the management of the business itself. In this context it is possible to identify three phases in the development of Total Quality, which can be classified as "generations" and that can be described as follows:

- *First generation*   Focused on the continuous improvement of manufacturing operations. The improvements are based on eliminating the causes of "non-quality" and waste. The pursuit of these objectives involves a large number of employees (normally organised in improvement groups) and is aimed at improving the "capacity" of the manufacturing processes (approaches often based on statistical process control), with a thrust which is mainly bottom-up. Most companies using Total Quality are still in this phase of development.
- *Second generation*   The increasing recognition that what can make a business truly competitive is substantial, continuous improvement both of its operating capacity and of its business processes (from new product development to invoicing), that is, the continuous improvement of the organisation of the business itself. This assumption leads to the introduction of more "managerial" features such as Management by Processes and Management by Policy (*Hoshin Kanri*). Throughout the world there are already many companies which have entered this phase of development (probably 5–10% of companies claiming to manage by Total Quality).
- *Third generation*   The "mature" phase of Total Quality. In companies which have reached this stage of maturity, Total Quality is essentially understood as being synonymous with management by priorities and by policy. Total Quality in these environments is considered to be a new, more effective

way of doing business, and its mechanisms are used to obtain a more entrepreneurial style of management. A small number of companies have reached this level of development. Among them one can think of a number of Japanese companies and a few of the leading firms in the West.

It is in this third generation of Total Quality that one can discern some of the approaches and "ingredients" illustrated in this book. I should like to stress, however, that what is proposed can, in a first phase, be totally independent from Total Quality. On the other hand, it is true that this approach will in itself generate a management culture which inevitably leads to developments, typical of Total Quality, such as management by priorities and by policy, as well as strong emphasis on the involvement of the employees of the firm. In particular it is true that the organisation of Breakthrough Management as it is proposed in this book is a first practical step towards the introduction of Management by Policy. However, it is equally true that the management instruments proposed can also make an important contribution in terms of effectiveness to companies which are already systematically using this new management system. They offer the means to "debureaucratise" its mechanisms, especially if (as in the majority of cases) they have been introduced following orthodox Japanese principles. This type of result, seen in several companies known for their advanced management methods, is for me the confirmation of the almost universal validity (dependent on management maturity) of the systems which are proposed.

I should like to thank all my colleagues in Galgano, especially Marco Diotalevi, Carlalberto Da Pozzo and Andrea Di Lenna, for their contribution to the methodologies described. My particular thanks also go to those many companies which have already translated this approach into concrete results. Finally, I want to thank Ralph Bullock whose professional contribution has been essential to this English edition and Daniela Pirovano for her precious assistance in the coordination of the book's translation.

1
What is Breakthrough Management?

By "breakthrough management" we essentially mean the capacity of a business quickly to achieve major operating results which are capable of ensuring its success both in the short and in the medium to long term. In other words, breakthrough management is the key to a firm becoming and remaining a business leader.

But what are these "major operating results"? They can be identified as "performance levels significantly higher than previously". In management jargon such leaps in performance are usually referred to as "breakthroughs". The first country to use the breakthrough concepts and approach on a large scale was Japan.

A good example of Japanese breakthrough capacity is Mitsubishi Heavy Industry: until 1985 this company managed to improve its non-quality costs by more or less 5% per annum; from 1986 onwards it succeeded in improving them at the rate of 50% per annum (without any particular investments)*. Two points are worthy of attention:

1 Since in a business concerned with major plant construction contracts, failure to comply with standards usually accounts for 20–30% of manufacturing costs, reducing non-compliance by 50% means a reduction in total costs of 10–15% in the first year (no worthless achievement!).

---

* Source: Ryuji Fukuda

2   What did this company do to change its capabilities so suddenly?

Let us confess that this capacity for improvement demonstrated by some Japanese companies has been for us the cause of considerable frustration in the not so distant past. In the West we were just not used to the systematic achievement of this sort of result. Our improvements were usually more random, and based on ingenious ideas and technological breakthroughs (often accompanied by heavy investments) rather than on the capabilities of operating managers.

Recently, however, these "Japanese" management capabilities have begun to make their appearance in a number of Western companies. Today Motorola, for example, declares that its quality improvement objectives are of the order of 90%, and IBM is at least as ambitious: at IBM-Semea in 1992, objectives included an improvement in quality of over 90% and a reduction in lead time of more than 50%. These are figures which were unthinkable only ten years ago, and even today would probably scare most managers as being apparently impossible. Yet these figures have become almost normal in some companies, and practically the rule in certain sectors.

Another example of European capacity in this field is given by Professor Ryuji Fukuda (breakthrough consultant to many Japanese and other companies). It is Sony. Sony began to introduce the breakthrough approach in 1987, focusing it on the priority of attacking "non-quality". By non-quality it meant anything wasted in production (in the Japanese approach, non-quality is anything which does not add value to the product).

Sony launched this programme simultaneously in all its plants worldwide—Japan, Wales, Stuttgart, France, Barcelona and at San Diego in California. The results of the new approach are illustrated in Figure 1.1. Taking as 100 the level of production non-quality in the European plants in January 1987, the Japanese plants were three times better. What happened during the years after the new approach was launched? Between January and December the European plants succeeded in raising their quality by 90–95%, while the Japanese "only" managed 50%. In the absolute these results are, of course, dramatic, but the case is particularly interesting since it also demon-

strates that in Europe it is possible to reach performance standards close to those of the best Japanese companies. Perhaps we
are not yet as good as they are at consolidating the results, but
in terms of effectiveness in achieving the priority targets we
have actually shown in this case that we can be better than the
Japanese.

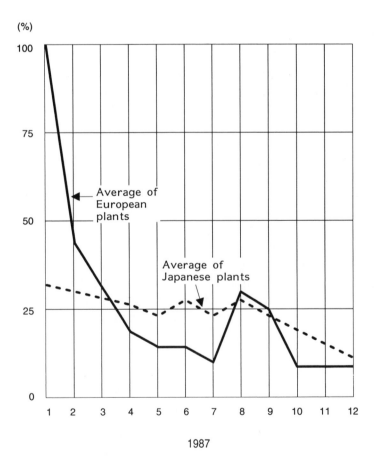

Figure 1.1   *The Sony TQM CEDAC programme. (Source: Ryuji Fukuda.)*

Table 1.1   Philips components—Bari factory results.

Results	1983	1985	1988	1989
Factory price (%)	100	89	81	75
Lead time (weeks)	5	4	3	2
CLIP (Committed Line Item Performance) (%)	80	100	100	100
Process rejects (%)	7.5	3	2	0.5
Finished products defects (ppm)	300	10	5	0.3
Customers complaints/year	100	15	9	2

Continuing with examples of breakthroughs, we can take the Bari plant of Philips Sud. In 1983 this plant was in competition with Philips Taiwan. "We have excess manufacturing capacity, and one of these plants has got to go. Let the best plant win." Bari managed to beat Taiwan. Ceramic condensers are still produced at Bari, Italy, but not in Taiwan.

Table 1.1 gives the results behind this success: a 25% reduction in manufacturing costs, complaints down from 100 to two per annum, defects in finished products down from 300 to 0.3 parts per million, process rejects from 7.5% to 0.5%, lead time from 5 to 2 weeks, and improvement in delivery reliability (CLIP) from 80% to 100% for 5 consecutive years. These were, of course, exceptional results, which Taiwan found impossible to achieve. Another particularly significant example is Michelin Italy. In the last few years this company has succeeded in making substantial improvements in its performance through a variety of coordinated actions, ranging from changes in the organisation through to the involvement of all its staff in the achievement of its business objectives.

As an example of the results achieved, one plant has been able to raise productivity by 10% per annum for four years running, and at the same time obtain improvements in quality, lead time, maintenance costs (−22%) and in flexibility (+55%). The previous improvement capacity of the plant, which was already one of Michelin's best worldwide, was around 4–5% per annum. The performance of this plant today is probably better than that of its top American and Japanese competitors.

Now let us take the case of a car manufacturer, Ferrari Auto. The priorities were "reduction of production stocks" in 1991 and "quality improvement" in 1993. The results obtained were 50% in twelve months and 80% in five months respectively (Figure 1.2). The size of the improvement, and the few months taken to achieve them, are a good example of breakthrough.

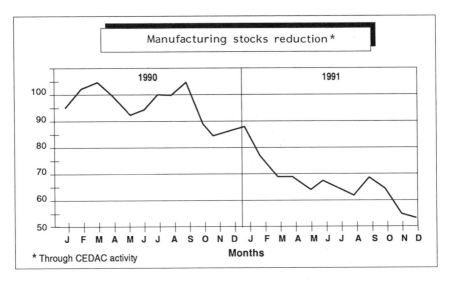

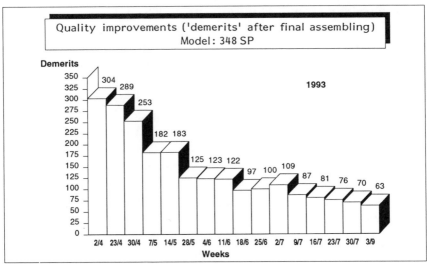

Figure 1.2 *Ferrari Auto (some breakthroughs).*

A final example of striking results obtained is Beretta (Italian manufacturer of wall boilers). They obtained reductions of 80% in rework, 60% in work in process, 50% in lead time, all in less than ten months.

These are all examples of breakthrough management. But how can we develop this capability? How can we achieve breakthrough management? There are certain prerequisites, certain "effectiveness factors" which must first be acquired. The first can be defined as the *capacity to choose the right objectives*. It would be a waste of time to achieve improvements of 80–100% in a particular area if these did not also translate themselves into a major improvement of overall business performance, or into a significant improvement of one of its competitive factors. The improvement must make its impact on the "right" lever.

The choice of the objective on which to focus is in fact a key moment in breakthrough management: it already represents most of the value of the total potential result. If a plant of Michelin can achieve productivity increases of over 10% per annum, it is probably because it knows how to use the right levers, as well as by being effective in taking action. In fact the main discriminating factor for success seems to be just that: knowing how to choose the best areas in which to intervene from among all those possible (in a Pareto logic), and knowing how to choose the right improvement objectives.

If the choice of operational objectives is probably the most critical moment in breakthrough management, the second effectiveness factor is the *planning of the right actions for their achievement*. The "right" actions do not mean "all possible actions". This would be a "budgetary" approach. "Right" means choosing out of all of the steps possible the ones which are the most important, and concentrating on getting major results out of them. This planning capability does not mean planning everything in the bureaucratic, accounting sense. I repeat that it is the capacity to plan the right things and the right ways for doing them: a small number of things, the most important ones, with major results.

Continuing with the process of breakthrough management, a third effectiveness factor is the management of the improvement actions planned, that is, the *capacity to convert objectives into results*. In many companies we see plenty of fine plans with poor results! They consist of plans which are well drawn up and sufficiently detailed . . . it is just a pity that they were not transformed into results!

In reality, if we were to analyse these plans, we should discover that they were not well thought out. Often, for example, they aim to tackle too many things at once, but only plan 5% improvements for everything. This is not entrepreneurial management! The real entrepreneur is the person who can spot those few levers which are really important to the result of the business, and can concentrate the firm's efforts on them to dramatic effect.

But even a good "entrepreneurial" plan may not yield the hoped-for results. As I said, many businesses actually fail when it comes to implementing their plans. Although they have been good at choosing the right objectives, they then go ahead and fail in the action phase. They are incapable of mobilising their own organisation effectively to pursue these objectives (they do not know how to convert objectives into results).

The last critical factor of breakthrough management (the fourth effectiveness factor) is *the capacity to convert the improvements obtained into irreversible, consolidated performance*, so that they do not degenerate later, and spoil the result originally achieved. This is where yet another number of businesses fail.

A business can therefore only be considered excellent if it is better than its competitors in each of these four effectiveness factors. By excellent, I mean a business leader with the capacity to make breakthroughs every year in its business success factors and therefore remain leader. The other firms, although they may be relatively good, cannot make the world class. That is, they are not capable of competing at world level. If they are still competitive, it is because they have an exclusive product or a niche market. The moment that they find themselves in a less protected situation there are not very many firms capable of demonstrating world class in terms of productivity and effectiveness.

In summary, breakthrough management consists of the greater *relative* capacity to manage breakthrough (compared to its competitors), that is, the ability:

- To choose the right objectives
- To make effective and coherent plans

- To convert planned objectives into results
- To consolidate the new levels of performance

But how can we set about developing these capabilities successfully? What are the essential requirements? This is the theme which we now develop.

SUMMARY

What does "breakthrough management" mean? It means the capacity to achieve important operating results (breakthroughs) such as:

- Increase productivity or reduce costs by at least 10% per annum
- Improve quality by 70–90% per annum
- Reduce lead time by 50% per annum

This is the result of the chain effect of specific "subsidiary" capacities (the four effectiveness factors):

- To identify the right objectives and "levers"
- To make an effective, coherent plan
- To convert objectives into results
- To consolidate the new levels of performance

2
The Basic Requirements of Breakthrough Management

THE APPROACH

Conceptually, operating effectiveness can be thought of as entrepreneurial capacity applied to managing. By entrepreneurial capacity we mean mainly the capacity to choose the real priorities of the business, to be coherent in their pursuit, and to be effective in their achievement. It is not by chance that when we examine firms in difficulty we regularly find weaknesses attributable to:

- Insufficient reaction to change
- Dispersion of effort on too many fronts
- Lack of operational coherence
- Poor operating effectiveness
- Incapacity to mobilise their employees on priorities

The distinctive characteristics of an effective management can be summarised by the following three key factors:

1 Effectiveness
2 Coherence
3 Mobilisation

This means that a firm will be really successful to the extent that it can apply these factors better than other competing firms. Indeed it is not possible in this context to measure good performance in the absolute since, as we well know, success comes from attaining positions of relative advantage. It is obvious that the greater the gap to be closed or the trend on which we must catch up, the greater are the risks involved in deciding which priorities we should concentrate on, and which are the objectives to be achieved.

But risk-taking has always been part of the entrepreneurial approach and behind great successes and major recoveries there has always been the acceptance of risk. Indeed, today there are really very few situations in which a business can afford the luxury of not taking risks. Where they do exist, they are in any case situations which cannot last for more than four or five years.

This was not true in the past, where, thanks to market conditions in which demand was greater than supply, it was sufficient to make small annual improvements in order to survive or even to be successful. These conditions unfortunately encouraged approaches based simply on "efficiency" or "optimisation" (an expression unknown to entrepreneurs) based on the respect of almost static standards which were actually considered optimal.

This logic also had an impact on the methods used for evaluating investments, so that the process became largely delegated to mathematical mechanisms for appraising their financial advantage, using only quantifiable "concrete" factors (the entrepreneur was replaced by computer programs!). This led inevitably to management cultures based on efficiency and specialisation, rather than on the development of entrepreneurial capabilities.

The mania for the optimisation of internal performance also meant that, over time, many businesses lost their ability to seize external opportunities, which led to irreversible losses of market share and, in consequence, of production volume. Yet even here it was possible for them, thanks to their managerial skills, to administer this downsizing without increasing losses. Indeed, these firms are usually good at working on costs. In fact, they only know how to work on costs. Paradoxically, they are even capable of making a profit out of withdrawing from business. Faced with such phenomena, it is better to state immediately that this book is not for that sort of firm, but for those who want to adopt an entrepreneurial approach. In this context the three factors already quoted of effectiveness, coherence and mobilisation take on the meaning which we now describe.

OPERATING EFFECTIVENESS

Operating effectiveness is concerned with the capacity of a firm to achieve major results in selected objectives. This characteristic is the result of other specific management capabilities (= "way of managing" = management system) recognisable through the following concepts:

- Continuous breakthroughs
- Management by priorities
- Visual management

Continuous Breakthroughs

In the successful, entrepreneurial firm, working by breakthrough (the pursuit of major improvement in a short period of time) is considered normal. This means that the firm is used to setting itself each year one or more highly challenging objectives on which to concentrate its efforts. Such a firm knows that it cannot afford the luxury of letting a year go by without making a breakthrough, on penalty of seeing a deterioration in its competitive position. The most "aware" companies have even introduced the concept of *break-even time* or *break-even trend* into performance improvement. They know that all their competitors are improving, and that an equivalent performance trend is therefore essential in order just to survive.

A trend slightly below the average of the competition implies difficulty in surviving, while a slightly better one immediately gives a competitive edge. A much poorer trend means risk of closure, a much better one guarantees success. Hence the need for careful *benchmarking* (comparison of performance with that of competitors), to decide on which priorities to set and what are the break-even points necessary (in time or trend).

One aspect to be considered is the fact that the same result may represent "competitive advantage" or simply the "cost of catching up with the competition", depending on whether it is achieved one year earlier or later (if two years later, it would probably not be enough to ensure survival!).

What, then, is the "necessary and sufficient" trend? It varies greatly from one sector to another, reaching values which were absolutely unthinkable a few years ago in the sectors where competition is at its hottest. The improvements themselves are, however, almost always concerned with the classic competitive factors, such as:

- *Time to market* (the time taken to develop and launch new products or execute an order)
- *Costs* (and therefore prices)
- *Quality* (conformity with purpose, in terms of "negative quality" and "positive quality")
- *Delivery* (i.e. the time taken in the supply chain from purchasing through to dispatch and service performance)

To be precise, C (costs), Q (quality) and D (delivery = dispatch and service) are the internal parameters by which Total Quality companies measure their business operating improvements (according to them if improvement cannot be measured in this way, it does not exist!). Another dimension recently introduced by Japanese firms as a specific requirement is the factor F = Flexibility (previously considered to be part of factor D).

Returning to the concept of breakthrough, as mentioned earlier, this varies considerably from sector to sector, being a "relative" factor. Below are a few examples of breakthroughs (expressed as Q, C, D, F factors) achieved by industry leaders (annual objectives, considered as break-even trends when set as priorities):

Computer and consumer electronic industries
Q   (negative quality)   = −50/90%
C   (costs)   = −15/20%
D   (lead time)   = −30/50%
Telecommunications and electromechanical industries
Q   (cost of quality)   = −30/50%

C (operating costs) = –10/15%
D (lead time) = –30/50%
Car industry
Q (defects) = –30/50%
C (product cost) = –5/10% (–30/50% over 3 years)
D (time taken by the logistic chain) = –30%

Management by Priorities

The breakthrough logic usually assumes that only one priority will be chosen per year (or per planning cycle, which may be as short as three months), but in some sectors or years, it may be necessary to set two or three breakthrough objectives at the same time. In any case, if we want to make breakthroughs, we must be capable of managing operations in a way which meets the requirements of maximum effectiveness. It is therefore necessary to introduce a regime of *exceptional management* for certain business (priority) objectives. "Exceptional" means requiring specific rules of the game, and therefore a focused organisation and *ad hoc* procedures.

For this, Japanese firms have developed an approach called Management by Policy, developed in the context of Total Quality Management. This is the successor to the original Management by Objectives, which is today considered to be relatively ineffective because:

- It had management performance appraisal as its principal objective, rather than business results in the absolute
- It was in fact a simple reflection of the budget
- It contained a large number of objectives (and was therefore dispersive)

In contrast, Management by Policy contains few objectives, but with target breakthroughs ("it is easier to achieve major results by concentrating on a small number of priorities than to pursue a whole variety of small objectives") and with a clear definition of policies (the "how", i.e. the *guidelines* much overlooked by Management by Objectives). A brief description of Management by Policy would seek to highlight the following main characteristics:

- Focus on a few basic priorities (one to three, periodically chosen by top management)
- Joint identification (by the people involved) of the objectives and the actions necessary to obtain the desired results (the "how" is more important than the "how much", since it conditions the future competitiveness of the business)
- A highly integrated, interfunctional process, focused on getting these results
- Synergy between the top-down and bottom-up processes
- Continuous, systematic management of the processes, aimed at the pursuit of the priority objectives
- Rigorous application of the PDCA method (Plan–Do–Check–Act)
- Emphasis on cause-and-effect relationships
- Direct audit by managers

A comparison between Management by Policy (MBP) and Management by Objectives (MBO) is given in Table 2.1.

One important feature of managing by priority is the relationship between the breakthrough objectives plan and the budget. As we all know, the budget is mainly concerned with results in terms of costs or volume (production, sales, etc.) which are usually analysed into cost centres. The breakthrough objectives plan is quite different. Although it may concern any type of objective, it is in fact limited strictly to the management of priorities, and concentrates on their operating characteristics rather than on accounting controls.

Another argument in favour of separating the management of the breakthrough plan from the budget is that the budget by its very nature must monitor expected levels of performance (to give standards which can be used for reviewing the overall cost structure and for setting standard costs). Therefore it is not possible for it to contain challenging objectives, since there is an element of uncertainty as to whether or not they will be achieved. If the two were not separated, we should end up with the usual bad habit of having two budgets (the "official" budget, containing challenging objectives, and the "real" cautious budget, used by management for its own evaluations), which often destroys the credibility of operating commitments.

Table 2.1 Comparison of MBP (Management by Policies) and MBO (Management by Objectives).

		MBO (Management by Objective)	MBP (Management by Policies)
1	Basics	• Behavioural theories • Scoring system	• Total Quality Control • Control cycle
2	Organisation	• Focused on the individual	• Focused on the organisation and groups of individuals
3	Operating system	• Decisions on objectives ("troubleshooting system") • Planning of the coherence between the objectives of the individuals	• "PDCA trouble-shooting cycle" • Management by processes • Top-down/bottom-up flows
4	Priority objectives	• Profits/costs • Objectives expressed in terms of profit and/or cost or volume	• Quality (customer satisfaction/fitness for purpose) • Global objectives on: quality, profit/cost/service
5	Approach and management	• Continuous pressure on objectives • Pragmatic approach: top-down or participative according to the needs	• Emphasis on processes and on flexibilities • Systematic participation by all

6	Evaluation of performance	• Based on results
		• Tied to personnel management
		  – Selection of the basis of results
		  – Evaluation of the job
		  – Score system
		  – Link with remuneration
			• Based more on "how" (process) than on results
			• Integrated into line management
			  – Audit by the director/ manager
			  – Self-evaluation of results/objectives differences
			  – Evaluation by "internal customers" and colleagues
			• No direct link with personnel management

7	Operating methods	• Based on "performance indicators" • The management of quality and industrial engineering are considered "sub-systems"	• Policy deployment system • Based on "control points" • The instruments of quality control and engineering are fundamental

Source: JUSE

There must, however, be a link between the breakthrough objectives plan and the budget; the latter must at least include the costs or allocation of resources planned as necessary for the achievement of the breakthrough objectives. When the breakthrough objective concerns costs, it is also possible to take account of it in the budget, but the following precautions must be taken:

1   The detailed indicators of an operating plan are based on what is possible to control in terms of operating management; they cannot coincide with the indicators of industrial cost accounting (which are mainly indicators of results). They must therefore be properly converted.
2   Since the breakthrough objectives plan must by its very nature be more ambitious than the budget (unless the performance target is the strict minimum required for the survival of the business), only a part of its objectives can be included in the budget (i.e. the most probable results).
3   Returning to the logic of breakthrough management, this presupposes the capacity to introduce an exceptional system for managing priorities, capable of a high degree of focus, that is:
    - A specific priorities management system
    - The use of *ad hoc* indicators
    - The overcoming of formal budget constraints

Visual Management

The final requirement for operating effectiveness is the capacity to use a "truly management" approach for the priorities chosen. It must be recognised that the management systems normally used by business tend to concentrate on management reporting rather than on the management itself. To understand the difference between management controlling through reports and actually managing is a basic requirement of breakthrough management. "Management control" essentially means periodic or spot checks on the actual results of operating performance compared with standards. "Managing" means *real-time supervision* of the performances on which the target results depend.

To make a comparison with driving a car, *management control* means checking that the actual usage and consumption per month or per day correspond with the budget (e.g. the actual mileage); managing means knowing the current actual performance of the car, its problems and opportunities for improvement, reacting accordingly and as quickly as possible (for example, by adjusting its speed). In other words, management controls appraise the average results produced (time taken, miles covered, consumption), whereas managers should be concentrating on managing the *variables in the process* which determine the results (the current speed, i.e the speedometer; the engine variables, i.e. the temperature and pressure gauges etc.; and, of course, the outside conditions such as the road, the weather etc.).

Therefore managing means to manage operations through the supervision and continuous improvement of the operating variables which determine management results. Management control, on the other hand, means "to compare actual results with what was forecast".

It is, moreover, obvious that supervising through the use of indicators, even monthly (that is, with only twelve opportunities per year to check them) cannot produce the level of effectiveness necessary to achieve a breakthrough. What is necessary above all is the capability to recognise and "manage in real time" those process indicators which can highlight improvements and drops in performance as they happen, and monitor the effectiveness of the improvement actions put in action without having to wait for confirmation that the final result sought has been achieved.

But real time is only achievable if the movement of the indicators in question is continuously on open display. This requirement is certainly not met if a report has to be consulted or, even worse, a meeting called. "Real time" is in fact synonymous with "visual management", that is, the capacity to evaluate what is happening through visual supports updated at high frequency and giving automatic signals. A computer monitor can meet this need if it displays trends in graphic form, but generally real "manual" graphic systems are used (although in reality highly computerised, as in NEC, Sony and Hewlett-Packard!).

COHERENCE

This refers to the capacity of a business to maintain a management approach which is capable of avoiding waste or contradiction of effort, creating synergy instead between action and its consequence over time. This capacity is the result of the operating coherence which management has been able to establish. This coherence can be seen in three dimensions:

1   Horizontal
2   Vertical
3   Strategic

Horizontal Coherence

Horizontal coherence is the result of the successful launch and execution of improvement actions so that all the functions and supervisors at the same level work substantially together in order to achieve the priority business objectives. Possible contradictions are eliminated at a higher level, to avoid the indiscriminate setting of objectives (the typical results of Management by Objectives when aimed at performance appraisal rather than operational effectiveness). The latter aproach would force every manager to give priority to pursuing *his or her own* objective, and refuse resources for a more important objective (belonging to someone else) or even oppose it.

The assignment of objectives (derived from a process of *deployment*—broken down and defined as indicators and targets to be managed) should in fact privilege the pursuit of the priority objectives, accepting that, depending on the priorities set for the year, the various managers and supervisors will be more or less involved in achieving these business objectives. Those who are less involved in the top-down priority objectives can concentrate more on the bottom-up objectives which they themselves propose (usually for solving the main problems of their own area). On the other hand, synergy must be ensured through joint responsibility for the most important objectives (the "red" objectives) and through the definition of policies which ensure that their actions are coherent.

Example of Incoherence Due to Lack of Policy Guidelines

1   General objective: 10% cost reduction
2   Second-level objectives:
   - Production director: reduce inspection and non-quality costs by 30%, reduce stocks by 30%
   - Purchasing director: obtain an 18% reduction in the price of purchased materials

Possible strategies for the production director are:

- Examine the possibility of eliminating incoming inspection
- Reduce the amount of in process and final inspections
- Reduce the cost of rework
- Reduce safety stocks (linked to quality problems)

Possible strategies for the purchasing director are:

- Seek purchasing economies through the use of purchasing power (but risking a degradation in the quality of the materials supplied)
- Stimulate competition by increasing the number of suppliers (but creating greater inconsistency in the materials supplied)
- Increase the lot size to obtain price discounts (increasing average stocks)

We can see the negative impact of the strategies of the purchasing director on the action planned by the production director, and in consequence the lack of coherence and the difficulties which will arise in the operations of this firm. Coherence would have been ensured by the prior definition of policy guidelines.

One example of a policy guideline which would avoid much of the incoherence seen in this case would be "valuation at full cost and not only by price". The operating policies which would then meet the objectives of the purchasing director, and also protect those of the production director, would be:

- Choose suppliers on the basis of the total costs generated by them, and not simply by price
- Reduce the number of suppliers, giving each of them more volume

- Obtain price discounts on the basis of the new economies of scale which they can achieve

It can be noted how these policies have a positive (synergetic) effect on the actions planned by the production director.

Vertical Coherence

The effectiveness of an improvement action programme is proportional to the number of actions or sub-objectives launched in synergy (the number of darts thrown at the same bull's eye). The concentration of all efforts on the same objectives is a basic principle of breakthrough management.

This would be grossly ignored if there was no coherence between the objectives down through the management structure. Indeed it is generally unacceptable that a subordinate should pursue an objective which is not the consequence of one of his or her superior's objectives. One of the two objectives would most probably not be related to the business priorities of the period. In any case, the objective of the superior would not be adequately supported at the operational level, and that of the subordinate would not be coordinated towards meeting objectives of the higher level.

The credibility of the management hierarchy itself would be at stake. I cannot convince a subordinate of the importance of his or her objective if at the same time I am busy with something quite different, even claiming that mine is more important! Vertical coherence ensures effectiveness both of the action itself and by motivating the staff (credibility, importance attached to the objective). It is precisely in the case of breakthrough objectives that deployment must penetrate to the lowest levels of the hierarchy, setting objectives for department and office managers, and even for individual operators if necessary.

Strategic Coherence

A business will be all the more successful to the extent that through its short-term actions, aimed at short-term objectives, it is also able to contribute to its medium- and long-term objectives. Let us suppose, for example, that a firm has chosen as a short-term objective the reduction of purchased material costs. Let us also suppose that it has at the same time chosen as a medium- to long-term objective (to acquire competitive advantage) the introduction of a "just-in-time comakership" organisation with its suppliers. To be strategically coherent in pursuing the reduction of purchasing costs, it absolutely must avoid short-term strategies such as "increase the number of suppliers" or "increase inspection activities".

In this case it would be following policies in contradiction to its medium- to long-term objectives, making it much more difficult to launch what has to be done afterwards (this firm would also have problems of credibility). Instead it should identify short-term policies in synergy with its medium- to long-term policies. That is, it should launch initiatives which also contribute to the future competitiveness of the business. In this case a policy which would contribute to both objectives would be, for example, to obtain lower prices by reducing the number of suppliers (and obtaining discounts in exchange for the larger volumes purchased). This would then already be contributing in the short term to the reduction in the number of suppliers indispensable to the implementation of the comaker strategy desired in the medium- to long-term.

The concept is illustrated in the vectors model in Figure 2.1. Vectors **A** and **B** represent the quantitative short-term objective. Vector **L** is the medium- to long-term objective. The possible directions of vectors **A** and **B** (the angles) represent alternative "means" ("how" policies) for achieving the same quantitative objective. Strategic coherence will obviously be greater if the short-term vector moves in the direction of the medium- to long-term vector. This is the case of situation **A**. On the other hand, situation **B** is a loser, since by pursuing the short-term objective in this way, the business is moving almost completely away from its medium- to long-term objective, not only failing to make any contribution to it but actually blocking it. A business is therefore effective if it is capable of ensuring coherence and synergy between its actions over time ("it knows how to line up its efforts").

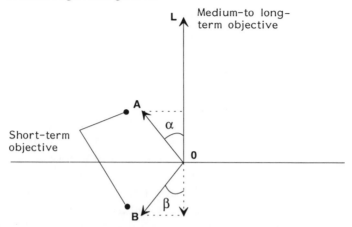

Figure 2.1 *Strategic consistency. 0A = 0B = short-term quantitative objective; α,β = alternatives in "how" (policies); A = synergistic situation; B = fighting situation.*

MOBILISATION CAPACITY

The capacity of a business to implement actions depends on its ability to stimulate the contribution of the people who "serve" or who can contribute to the priority objective in an organised, swift and effective way. Participation is already recognised as an essential requirement for managing a business today, but it becomes the principal competitive factor when it is a matter of tackling business priorities. In this context, "mobilisation" of a firm's resources will be all the more effective if it can meet the following requirements:

● Capacity to focus on priorities
● Intensive involvement of line management
● Intensive improvement activity

Focus on Priorities

Mobilising staff to achieve non-priority objectives presents two risks:

1 It takes resources away from priorities
2 The costs may exceed the benefits.

Although it is true that a Total Quality firm must promote bottom-up improvements in all its activities as well without first making a financial appraisal of them, it is also true that this can only be a subsidiary activity, involving resources not committed to priority improvements. For this reason it is extremely important to identify which are the priorities and the resources to be committed, through careful planning of the operations and of the types of action necessary ("policy-objectives deployment").

The priority objectives and sub-objectives ("red" to distinguish them from the others) must then receive particular emphasis, in terms both of organisation and of management. We must therefore put into place an organisation and an operating management system capable of taking on board the "exceptional" management necessary to achieve the priority objectives.

As mentioned earlier, an *ad hoc* organisational mechanism used by leading Japanese firms is Management by Policy. For operational control it will also be necessary to use other *ad hoc* indicators, perhaps currently dormant, or tailor-made to meet the criteria already described for visual management. The focus of all the staff on the priorities is sustained operationally through the intensive use of visual management mechanisms concentrated on the improvements defined in the "red" objectives (the SEDAC system, used by most of the breakthrough firms quoted in the Introduction, is a methodology developed for this purpose).

Intensive Involvement of Line Management

Mobilisation is more effective when it is led by the line organisation rather than by "lateral" structures or programmes. In a breakthrough management logic it would, moreover, be unthinkable to suppose that the line could have operating objectives different from those generated by the business priorities or, even worse, that it should not be the prime mover in setting up and managing the projects and actions which aim at achieving those priority objectives. This principle has two implications:

1   Priorities should be deployed so far as possible through the line organisation or through *Process Owners* (where Management by Processes is also used).

2   The use of organisational formula such as "interfunctional project groups" should be as limited as possible (only for set-up or for innovation projects).

So far as the second point is concerned, it is worth noting what happens in firms with an excellent improvement capacity. As a reference point, a firm can be considered excellent at improvement (according to a standard extrapolated from the best European experience) when it succeeds in producing a volume of improvement activity of the order of 300–400 targets or projects per annum for every 500 employees. This sort of performance is achieved through three basic types of improvement activity:

1   Activities managed in the line by working supervisors
2   Activities given as personal tasks to specialists
3   Activities carried out by interfunctional project/improvement groups (although often under individual leadership).

Taking as 100% the total of the improvement activities of a business, in excellent firms they are carried out as follows (averages extrapolated from an investigation made by Galgano & Associates):

- 70–80% by direct action in the line (type 1)
- 10–20% by personal tasks (type 2)
- 5–10% by group projects (type 3)

Type 3 is normally used when innovative solutions or improvements are required; type 2 for projects which are strictly specialist or of restricted scope; type 1 for everything considered to be capable of improvement on the ground, acting on existing processes. As can be seen, "excellent" firms have understood that only in a few cases (on average, 5–10%) is it advisable to have recourse to innovative remedies—usually for technological organisational problems. It must, however, be borne in mind that these activities, although statistically limited, account for over 20% of the total improvement obtainable (since they have greater "leverage") and are therefore far from negligible.

Similar results were obtained in a study of five world-class "excellent" firms carried out by Ryuji Fukuda; these results are given in Tables 2.2 and 2.3. The improvement categories indicated as B and C are those which by their very nature are or should be carried out by line management (type 1). Category D, which are issues requiring major change, imply frequent

Table 2.2 Types of problems/improvement opportunities.

Company Category	T	X	Y	W	Z
B	50	45	50	35	50
C	40	30	35	30	45
D	10	25	15	35	5
Total (%)	100	100	100	100	100

Definitions
Category B: The right method is established and understood by all concerned, but there are some individuals who do not practise it properly
Category C: The right method is established, but there are some individuals who are not informed of it properly
Category D: The right method is not established, no one knows it at the moment
T Japanese steel company
X Japanese electronics company
Y European car company
Z European chemical company

Table 2.3 How to tackle problems/improvement opportunities.

Type of problem/ opportunity	Aver- age %	Way to approach	Responsibility/ organisational body
Cat. B	46	• Training • Error causes analysis • Visual management/ foolproofing • Skill analysis	• Line managers and staff • Study groups • Individual assignments
Cat. C	36	• Communication • Training	• Line managers and staff • Study groups • Individual assignments
Cat. D	18	• Changes in operational methods (80%) • Innovation in operational methods (20%)*	• Line managers • Study groups • Individual assignments • Project groups

* Improvement by innovation/project groups = 20% of 18% = 3.6% of the whole improvement activity volume

recourse to "projects" (types 2 and 3). According to this study the need for real innovation, where it is essential to set up organised interfunctional project groups, is limited to 3.6% of cases.

Given that the major part of improvement activities can be directly implemented by the line organisation (about 80% of the total improvements) it is obvious that the capacity of middle-level line managers to carry them out becomes a key factor. An organisation will be all the more effective if its middle managers are capable of systematically stimulating and managing the involvement of their subordinates and other functions in the pursuit of the "red" objectives of the firm.

Intensive Improvement Activity

Two basic considerations are:

1   The size of the improvement depends on the volume of activity developed
2   The speed of the improvement depends on the "intensity" of the activities.

A breakthrough improvement is also distinguished from a normal one by the relatively short time taken to achieve it. An improvement of 10% in a year is a small improvement; the same improvement in a week is an excellent one.

To obtain breakthrough results we must be capable of carrying out a large volume of activities at high intensity in terms of time. A quality leap consists of succeeding in making improvement an ordinary, routine activity; that is, an activity to be carried out regularly on a daily basis, alongside traditional daily work. Improvement through spasmodic activities such the "weekly meeting" is certainly not sufficient to generate the volumes of improvement necessary and the types of results which we are discussing. This is the reason for limiting as far as possible the use of organisational formula which by their very nature require "on-off" type activities and a great deal of coordination, organisation and formal meetings (such as programmed project groups). Instead we must use methods which can operate continuously and interact openly under the management of the line structure.

To implement breakthrough management we must make improvement happen continuously every day. In excellent firms, particularly in Japan, improvement has become the most important daily activity (not necessarily in the amount of time taken up, but certainly as a commitment and a management priority). Once this strategic priority is accepted, the problem becomes organisational: how to launch a "breakthrough" approach to management which is capable of operating as a matter of routine. This book also aims to answer this question.

SUMMARY

The effectiveness of operating management is an entrepreneurial quality. The distinguishing feature of entrepreneurial management is the capacity to be effective and coherent at the same time. But the major results are achieved through the ability to mobilise "the people who can contribute" to the pursuit of these objectives. Effectiveness, coherence and mobilisation capacity are therefore three key factors in breakthrough management.

However, the "effectiveness" requirement can only be satisfied if:

- The objectives are genuinely "breakthrough"
- We are capable of "managing by priorities"
- A real-time "visual" system is installed for managing the performance indicators linked to the breakthrough objectives

The "coherence" requirement presupposes the capacity to be coherent in the following ways:

- Between the operating objectives of the various units/ supervisors (horizontal coherence)
- Between the objectives and actions of the management structure (vertical coherence)
- Between actions over a certain timespan (strategic coherence)

Only a firm with these characteristics can achieve the level of synergy between the various people and actions concerned which is necessary to ensure that its improvement activities are coherent and effective.

The "mobilisation capacity" requirement means:

- To be able to focus on the priorities
- To be capable of activating a high level of involvement of line managers
- To be able to develop a large volume of improvement activities

3
The Effective Planning Process

INTRODUCTION

As discussed earlier, the effectiveness of management depends above all on its ability to identify the most important objectives on which to concentrate. Moreover, it would be deplorable to waste time and precious resources on unimportant objectives. Results obtained in such conditions, even if excellent, would not be capable of having a significant influence on the bottom line. We have also seen the importance of managing the right compromise between short- and medium- to long-term priorities. The identification of the priority objectives and of the actions required to pursue them is the main task of business planning, from strategic through to operations planning.

What are the planning characteristics required to ensure effective management? How can we identify priority objectives and supporting actions? How do we formulate an effective plan? This chapter aims to start answering these questions, and to examine the planning process in the following phases:

- The choice of priority objectives and the compromise between short- and medium- to long-term objectives (the "mix" problem)
- The strategic planning process
- The preparation of the operating plan

THE CHOICE OF PRIORITY OBJECTIVES

The choice of the objectives for which to set up breakthrough management is the crucial moment in a planning process. To be the "right" one, an objective must satisfy certain criteria and have certain characteristics. To summarise concepts already discussed, it must, above all, be a *priority* objective. If it does not concern an issue important to the business it will not be an objective capable of generating major business results.

This concept may seem banal, but it is worth stressing. In firms which use Management by Objectives in a bureaucratic way, the choice of objectives is often guided more by the need to set objectives for everyone than by the overriding theme of identifying the business priorities and the means to pursue them. In these firms the business plan is more an accounting exercise than a business plan worthy of the name. In it there are no objectives which unequivocally take precedence over all others at company level. Paradoxically there is instead an attempt to give objectives to all the managers, with the risk of creating situations in which they can block priority business objectives simply by pursuing the specific objectives set for them (through "ignorance" of the priorities and because they are appraised exclusively on the achievement of their own objectives). Because of requirements which could be called aesthetic and because of performance appraisal, there is the risk that an objective worth "one" to the business is given the same attention as an objective worth "ten" given to another manager (for each of them, their own objective is the most important).

A second requirement that objectives must respect in order to ensure effective management has been identified as *coherence*. We must be able to ensure at the planning stage that there are no conflicts between actions aimed at the short term and those aimed at the medium- to long-term.

Another requirement of the objectives for breakthrough management is the practical possibility of being able to pursue them, that is, their *"manageability"*. In this context, as we have already seen, they must be monitored through indicators which are different from those used in management reporting or in financial accounting. It is in fact rare that even the form of the latter is of much use in day-to-day management.

An example. If we want to improve the quality of a product in market terms, what we are probably trying to obtain is a reduction in the number of complaints and of technical assistance visits. Therefore these are the indicators that we must use to evaluate the results, since it is these that can confirm that the improvement has actually taken place. But to pursue this objective we must take certain specific actions and make a number of changes. Unfortunately, the indicators just mentioned are of little use to operating management. They can only be measured after a considerable lapse of time (perhaps 6–12 months). We cannot check that we are doing the right things if we have to wait so long! Although it is true that we can and must summarise the results in these terms, it is also true that to supervise the actions necessary for the achievement of the objective we must use more "direct" means.

We must find *operating indicators*, with a faster feedback and linked to the specific actions launched, which can provide continuous data on how product quality is improving as a result of what is being done. For example, quality measured at the end of the line, quality sampled in production, or better still, indicators of the process variables on which final quality depends, and which presumably we are working on to achieve the desired results.

Returning to the theme of the choice of priority objectives, the process of identifying them through the analysis of their coherence and their "manageability" is certainly the basic feature of effective planning. The winning plan is the one which guarantees a business a high cash flow in the short term but also competitiveness in the medium to long term. The company which takes out too much in the short term prejudicing its future is a loser, as is the one which ignores short-term results while pursuing medium- to long-term success (in the meantime, it closes down!). A high level of *coherence and synergy between actions over a period of time* is therefore necessary.

But, as we well know, the planning and management scenario is disturbed by another dimension, *emergencies*, which by definition are unplannable. The effective approach is the one which reconciles the capacity to manage emergencies with the need to meet the financial objectives of the future. For this we need what we may call an "entrepreneurial" approach capable of identifying those priorities and policies which can ensure operating coherence over time.

Speaking of entrepreneurs, I like to think that the Italians are perhaps the best entrepreneurs in the world taken as individuals. Indeed, so long as a business can be managed by a single individual, there is no shadow of a doubt that the best business in the world is Italian. But when the business grows in size, entrepreneurs run into great difficulties if they do not change their management style. They can no longer manage everything "visually" by themselves as they had the habit of doing in their small businesses. The organisational machine takes off, and then the large Italian firms are no longer among the best in the world (not the worst, but certainly not the best).

The entrepreneurs in the large Italian company, probably "assisted" by general managers, do not seem to be able to remain effective when they have to filter through a complex organisation. Let us say that in general they find it more difficult than a number of their foreign colleagues.

On the other hand, it is the Japanese who distinguish themselves in the management of major firms. And yet their capacity as entrepreneurs and individualists is small. It is no accident that Japanese small businesses exist in practice only because they are launched by and fed with work from major industries as their "appendages". But in that case, how on earth do the managers of the major Japanese firms manage to be so entrepreneurial? It is as if they had managed to extract the essence of the entrepreneur and distil it into a system which succeeds in turning ordinary managers into entrepreneurs. The result is that they succeed in working by priorities although they are in a large firm and part of a big system, just as our entrepreneurs would do in their small businesses. It is precisely for this reason that the Japanese developed and implemented Management by Policy.

But what is this entrepreneurial approach that I am talking about? As I said earlier, it consists of the ability to pursue effectively and *at the same time* objectives with three different horizons (short, medium and long term) and also manage emergency situations. This means the simultaneous management of actions which will have their impact at different points in time (Figure 3.1)

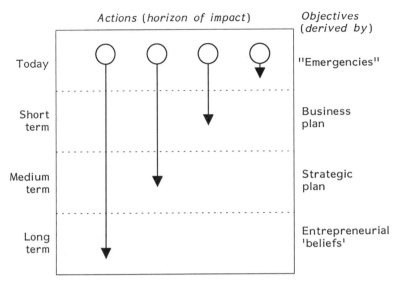

Figure 3.1 Relations between objectives/results and actions.

The entrepreneurial characteristics mainly treated in this book are those of operating management. The basic capacities necessary in this context are:

- To manage emergencies effectively and coherently
- To manage effectively and coherently the priority objectives derived from the annual business plan (identified as short-term objectives)
- To manage effectively and coherently the medium-term priority objectives (normally derived from the strategic plan)
- Finally, to manage effectively and coherently the future of the business (whose objectives are not derived from any strategic plan but from the "creed" of the business)

The last requirement reminds us of Japanese entrepreneurs, who claim that they plan their business over 10–11-year horizons. How do they do it? They certainly do not plan in figures over 10 years! Instead they plan their "creeds". Examples of these are flexibility, customer satisfaction, the cultivation of global managers instead of specialists, etc. The fact that such policies will improve the financial results of the firm cannot be demonstrated mathematically, but entrepreneurs know it, "they believe it".

The Japanese are highly capable planners of precisely this sort of thing. They call it "long-term policies". In the Western world, on the other hand, we find planning policies difficult. Instead we frequently call "strategic plans" three- or five-year plans in which we attempt to plan figures representing expectations or objectives (usually financial or, at most, market share and volumes related). Another problem of traditional Western firms is that very often they plan the same types of performance for the year and for the medium term, that is, using the same indicators projected over different horizons, although with different levels of aggregation. Let us now look at a few examples which illustrate what I mean by emergencies, short-, medium- and long-term objectives (Table 3.1).

The **emergency** normally consists of problems to be solved or opportunities to be seized. They are something which must absolutely be faced or resolved at top speed.

Examples of emergencies are a factory stoppage, an invitation to tender, a complaint from an important customer. More generally it is something to be "caught on the wing", a "take it or leave it" or more often, a "big problem to be resolved". In these situations there is no scientific method to be applied. Here competitive advantage depends on the capacity for improvisation, for quicker reaction than the others (in these cases the West excels).

Table 3.1   Examples of objectives by "horizon".

Emergencies	Short term	Medium term	Long term
• Removal of problems • Seizing of opportunities Examples: – Quality problem – Process breakdown – Customer complaint – Important bid – . . .	• Improvement of operational performances Examples (indicators): – Costs – Revenues – Process quality – Volumes – Market share – Productivity – Stocks – Cash flow – . . .	• Improvement of capabilities of operational performances Examples (indicators): – Lead time – Time to market – Process capability – Flexibility – Customer satisfaction • "Technological improvement" • . . .	• Improvement of strategic capabilities • Human Resources capabilities • Technological breakthroughs • Market strategies • . . .

Now let us look at some examples of **short-term objectives.** These are usually objectives aimed at the *improvement of operating performance, impacting on current year financial results.* For example, reduce costs by 10%, improve quality by 40%, increase sales by 5%, reduce order-filling time by 50%, increase production volume by 20%, increase market share by 3%, increase productivity by 15%, reduce stocks by 30%. These are common examples of annual objectives set by companies today.

What then are **medium-term objectives?** They are those objectives which *ensure that the business will still be competitive in 2–3 years' time.* What are they concerned with? Usually *improvements to the capabilities of the organisation* which will have an impact on its competitiveness; that is, improvements which will only be reflected in terms of financial results after a few years.

The problem of identifying medium-term priorities lies in the difficulty of understanding where the business is potentially exposed to competition in a scenario projected two or three years hence, and in deciding which features of competitive advantage should be concentrated on in such a scenario. Among the objectives which aim at medium-term competitiveness, we often find time to market, that is, new product development time. It is obvious that the reduction of this sort of timescale will only have an impact on business results after a number of years. It will only become evident when the new product begins to generate higher revenues than competitive products, thanks to its level of "relative" innovation.

Another frequent typical medium-term objective is the reduction of lead time. An example of this type of objective would be the capability to manufacture and deliver a product within two weeks from receipt of order, whereas previously it was only manufactured against sales forecast (which only allowed delivery two months after receipt of order). Even this type of advantage can only be exploited effectively in the marketplace after suitable marketing, probably not before the following year.

A further example of a medium-term objective is customer satisfaction. It is clear that satisfied customers today mean a guarantee of another order the next time round (the time cycle depends on the type of product). In contrast, taking undue advantage of the customer is an example of a bad short-term objective: it ensures the best possible result for the current year, but a loss of market share in the following years. How many firms could tell the tale of how they took advantage of customers to make the maximum out of them for a year, and then lost market share over the medium term!

Other examples of medium-term objectives are improvements in technology or in process capabilities, and improvements in quality of service.

So far as **long-term objectives** are concerned, the basic question to help identify them is "what will our company be in 5–10 years' time?" The Japanese reply would be "it will be exactly what the firm's employees are able to make it; it will be the result of their capabilities and nothing else". This implies that the process of developing new senior and middle managers and new workers becomes very important. We must concern ourselves today with developing the right people who will know how to carry us forward in the future in the direction in which we wish to go. If we are thinking of a future where the firm must be more "flexible", we must be sure to develop a culture of flexibility, and not one of functional specialisations.

If we want a businesss with a great capacity for sensing and understanding market needs, we must create the capacity to decode weak market signals. This capacity is linked with a certain type of person, but also with certain types of instrumentation and organisation (for which we must start planning today). There may also be issues of technology, or a combination of technology and market.

Once these factors have been identified, we must decide and plan how to pursue them. As Toyota rightly says, "Before producing products, we must produce the right people. The products are no more than the result of the capabilities of the people".

Let us consider those firms which start by deciding on what they want to produce, then about the organisation required, and finally about the people that they must find. This process is back to front, more suited to milking a business in the short to medium term than to preparing it to be a long-term winner.

To be precise, the organisational and cultural shape which we want to create over the long term is today commonly termed "vision". The vision represents the image of the firm which we should "like" to create over the next 5–10 years. It represents what we consider to be the winner for the future. It is usually expressed as a "desired state" through guiding principles, policies, types of organisation with reference to the operating capacities of the firm, such as: maximum customer satisfaction, flexibility, learning organisation, flat structure, management by process, management by policy, simultaneous engineering, etc. The objectives, and in consequence the actions to be taken to pursue this vision, can then be defined as "long-term objectives". A large part of them depends on the development of the capabilities of people, so it is understandable that a 5–10-year planning horizon is necessary in order to achieve them.

Returning to the classification of objectives into the three timescales of short, medium and long term, from the viewpoint of planning its practical importance is that to ensure the success of a business we must be able to plan and implement simultaneous, effective actions which make their impact on three horizons, using the right mix of effort. Indeed, since we cannot supervise hundreds of short-, medium- and long-term objectives, we must limit the number and choose just a few . . . the most important ones. We must also decide how much effort and cash it is right and opportune for us to invest in the short, medium and long term, in our own business and at a given moment in time. The answer depends on one or two basic considerations.

The problem of mix, that is, how much resource/commitment/ effort to dedicate to objectives over the three horizons, is indeed a critical moment in the planning process. It has a major impact on the choice of the number of objectives and on their nature (Figure 3.2). Yet there is no scientific method for tackling such a problem. However, it is possible to give a few points of reference.

In broad terms it could be said that a "normal" business steaming ahead in calm waters should be fairly concerned with the short term, but should be particularly concerned with ensuring its success in two or three years' time. It is therefore on this horizon that it should mainly be concentrating. On the other hand, a business with major short-term problems can certainly not afford to lower its guard on its current operating results. It is clear that for this type of firm the level of effort will be greater for the short term than for the other horizons. It would, however, be a mistake to conclude that this type of firm cannot afford the "luxury" of choosing any medium- to long-term priority objectives because it cannot dedicate resources to them.

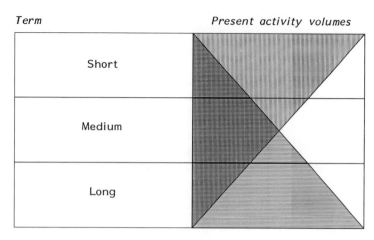

Figure 3.2   The "mix" problem.

In reality, so far as medium- to long-term objectives are concerned, this firm should be even more "entrepreneurial" and aware than the others. Since it can dedicate only limited resources to the medium to long term, it must have a very clear idea of what is most important. It must choose very accurately, since it cannot commit itself to very many objectives. One will be more than enough and it will already be an effort to pursue it. It must be the right one.

It is not therefore true that a business with short-term difficulties should be managed by someone who is only good at rigorous short-term action. Unfortunately, this firm needs two types of management capacity: high short-term effectiveness and also highly entrepreneurial skills so as to choose the right medium- to long-term priorities. It is precisely because it cannot fight on many fronts that it must find one single medium- to long-term priority. It must take great risks.

Yet the most common mistake made by the firm in short-term difficulties is to cut out all medium- to long-term expenditure or investment, with the excuse that it must concentrate entirely on its short-term problems. If this is applied indiscriminately to all its objectives entirely or even partially, the future of the firm is easy to foresee. It will carry on limping along, with a new emergency every year, until finally one year is a complete failure. At this point it will be forced to close.

The reason for this inevitable fate is obvious: how could this business be competitive two or three years later if it had invested nothing to achieve this competitiveness? Perhaps the market will be ready to halt for three years and wait for it? Certainly not! But then, if there is no sense in cancelling all investments in the future, reducing them all in proportion is also a losing strategy. The result would still be a mediocre firm, which could not survive for long in today's markets. The only valid solution for this firm is to have the courage to invest what little it has by concentrating on a single competitive factor on which to build the future. The choice is very difficult, but also very important.

The final reference model is the company which is highly profitable and in a strong leadership position (that is, with a strong advantage over its competitors). This situation can arise from the competitive advantage of having a product which the others do not have (product leadership) or because it is much better organised (for example, making what the customer needs very quickly to order) or through technological leadership. This type of firm can certainly afford the luxury of thinking more about the future than the present, particularly since it is running no risks for the next two or three years because of its privileged position. It should therefore be thinking about what to do so that it is still leader five or six years later and work intensively on these factors.

If this firm started to milk the product like a short-term cash-cow, it would certainly make large profits today, but within a few years would probably be in difficulty. It should therefore be dedicating its resources more to maintaining its position of leadership than to squeezing the maximum out of its competitive advantage.

In conclusion, the choice of objectives should be based on the following questions:

1   What volume of effort should I commit to each of the three management horizons (strategic mix)?
2   What are the priority objectives for the three horizons?

Confirmation that this is the way that world leaders already work comes from Xerox, a top reference both in the United States (winner of the Malcolm Baldrige Quality Award) and in Europe (where Rank Xerox was winner of the first European Quality Award in 1992). It has defined its priority objectives as return on assets for the short term, market share for the medium term and customer and employee satisfaction for the long term. The two operating objectives (ROA and market share) are carefully planned, launched and managed by the affiliates through the use of the Management by Policy and Policy Deployment mechanisms. The result of this deployment is the management operating plan.

Returning to the effective planning process, for maximum operating effectiveness the ideal would be to have only one important objective each for the short and medium term, and a few policy guidelines for the long term (like Xerox). A clear indication of the "major priority" can be of further help (also according to David T. Kearns, CEO of Rank Xerox).

But the reality is that we are going to have to supervise our objectives simultaneously (at least two operationally: the short and medium term). The problem then becomes how to manage and how to measure them. If we cannot decide on what is meant by improvement, how it is measured and supervised, and how we can ensure that it is taking place, we cannot talk about managing improvement.

The choice of the priority objectives and their indicators is one of the main outputs of the effective planning process. We will now see how the criteria described are transformed into formal plans.

STRATEGIC PLANNING

Introduction

We treat the theme of strategic planning in the context of the logic and methods typically used by large firms. The approach presented can be considerably simplified for firms (usually small or medium sized) which have not really formalised their own strategic planning process. But it must in any case be "lean" and concrete rather than formal (this is also true of large firms). The principles and logical phases described below are in any case basic essentials for entrepreneurial management, whatever the size of the firm (only the degree to which they are formalised should vary).

The Reference Pattern

Strategic planning in an entrepreneurial mode can be called "global strategic planning", where the adjective "global" emphasises its differences compared with the methods previously used. The global strategic plan encompasses the normal strategic plan (if it exists, otherwise it is sufficient to refer to objectives considered to be strategic), but it also has other aspects which are not normally included in the planning process. In addition, it projects the planning horizons of organisational development beyond the 3–5 years normally used.

The starting point for its preparation is the existing strategic plan, which is usually concerned with items such as market share, revenues, costs, investments, product/market strategies, etc. It is enlarged to include other basic planning ingredients: *the reference model* for business development, and *self-assessment* (see Figure 3.3).

The *reference model* looks at the development in organisation planned by the firm to realise its vision and defines the logical phases involved and their timing. It contains the organisational, strategic and cultural principles which constitute the

Figure 3.3 *Global strategic planning.*

"development policies" of the business, to which everyone must refer in pursuing their own objectives (the level of formalisation of the context and the extent to which it is broken down depend on the culture of the firm concerned).

This means that everything of importance which has been planned by the firm for the years covered by the plan must be "mapped out" on this model, which can be used as a "grid" (see below). It will be used as an *instrument panel* for the planning and management of all the business, ensuring coherence between its sub-systems and the "graduality" of its implementation.

The organisational *self-assessment*, on the other hand, consists of the management of the company identifying the major current and potential future issues to be faced by the business. This evaluation is projected into a business scenario covering three to five years. The output of this self-assessment is a fundamental step towards identifying priorities for action in organisational, cultural, technical or methodogical areas (the "how" priorities).

The global planning approach also introduces a "policy" environment to the whole planning process through the application of policy guidelines: *the long-term policies*. These policies are defined and announced by the chairman/managing director of the company and contain values connected with the *mission* of the firm and its long-term *vision*. In Japanese firms, for instance, these are taken as the primary reference for planning and for operating management.

We will now describe in greater detail how to prepare a reference model and carry out self-assessment.

The Reference Model (the Grid)

The development reference model, from now on referred to as the "grid" from its suggested shape, should be drawn up independently by each firm, taking account of its own culture, technologies, market and the specific characteristics of its own operating environment. It should have two dimensions (Figure 3.4):

1   The logical development phases
2   The subsystems to be supervised or developed

Subsystems / Phases	A	B	C	...	...	...	...	Z
1								
2								
3								
...								
...								
...								
n								

Figure 3.4   *The reference model ("the grid").*

The logical development phases are then converted into a time programme linked to the strategic plan. For each development phase, a specific organisational and technical configuration is defined for implementation in each sub-system.

Once prepared, the grid allows the firm to steer the development of the organisation coherently towards the vision, through the management and control of the "development front" (the line which represents the degree of implementation of the plan). This front must be managed with great sensitivity if a successful programme is to be developed (Figure 3.5).

The number of development levels included in the grid usually varies between three and seven, and the number of sub-systems between six and thirteen (data extrapolated from approximately 50 cases). There are usually three categories of sub-system:

A   Principal operating processes
B   Business culture, organisation and management
C   Methodologies and instruments required

and four logical/time phases:

0   Present situation
1   First development phase (clearly defined)
2   Second development phase (indicative)
3   Vision (desired state)

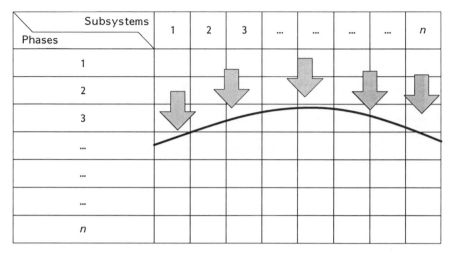

Figure 3.5   *Development by a "coherent" front.*

The phases and therefore their content are of the *rolling* type: they are systematically updated (annually or by development phase). This means that intermediate configurations will be progressively extracted from the vision, and that the vision itself will be progressively updated and projected forward in time with a new, more "advanced" content. Here is an example of a breakdown of the three categories of sub-systems:

A   *Principal operating processes*:
Customer/market relationships
Product development and engineering
Supply chain/suppliers relations
Manufacturing
B   *Culture, organisation and management*:
Company culture
Management role
Organisation and management systems
Employee relations
C   *Methodologies and systems*:
Improvement organisation (Total Quality)
Principal improvement activities
Basic methodologies
Quality system and procedures.

An example of a company grid is given in Table 3.2. (In small/medium-sized firms or in "simple" businesses, the breakdown of the grid can be reduced.) The boxes in the grid are usually simple statements of principle, or even slogans. They are definitions which aim to identify an operating pattern to be implemented in that phase or on that sub-system. These are broken down and defined in greater detail for the first development phase. They help management and those who are involved in the development of the plan to have an overall vision, almost a "visual supervision" of the developments necessary.

But for the development of the individual sub-systems more detailed working definitions are required. For each box there is a *zoom*, an explosion of the reference criteria and practical, detailed working explanations of the slogans contained in the general grid. This is again broken down for the first stage of development. The grid is drawn up by top management whereas the detailed breakdown of the reference criteria is carried out by interfunctional working groups composed of the managers of the various functions involved in supervising the sub-system or the process in question.

In the largest firms it is often necessary to insert further levels in the grid (lower-level grids) in order to arrive at the level where there are the elements necessary for the setting up of the implementation plan. An example of the breakdown of a grid of a large firm into three levels would be:

1 Company grid
2 Division grid
3 Operating unit grid (for example, plant, workshop or selling subsidiary) or for each basic process (for example, production or logistics)

It is worth recalling that the grid must take account of all the important actions having an impact on the organisation which the firm intends to launch in the future, whatever their motivation or purpose (obviously only those envisaged or actively considered as possibilities). This is then reviewed annually or at the end of each development phase.

The grid offers top management a great opportunity to review its plans, and also their coherence. In fact, by using this

Table 3.2   Company grid example.

Development levels	Relationship with customer	Relationship with suppliers	Manufacturing	Logistics	Product development and industrialisation	Quality culture
Level 0 (Initial situation)	• The quality level of the product/service is the result of the internal culture • Attention only to complaints *"Product out"* *"Service out"*	• Large number of suppliers • Systematic incoming inspection • Priority to prices	• Priority to direct costs • Optimisation through sub-systems	• Programming by functions • Optimisation by sub-systems	• Quality equals conformity with technical specification • Emphasis on "negative" quality • Process fragmented across a number of functions with progress regulated by procedures	• Quality equals product quality • The quality level is controlled by norms and standards • Specialist technical approach to quality
Level 1 (Continuous improvement capability)	• Improvement of products/service • Organisation for customer satisfaction • Bench-marking on customer satisfaction • Monitoring customer satisfaction *"Product in"* *"Service in"*	• Selection/reduction number of suppliers • Pilot JIT area • Purchases and vendor rating on price quality service • Launch auto certification • Programme ordering • Launch comakership	• Priority to total costs • Organisation by flows • Job enlargement • JIT organisation (MRP–kanban) • Total productive maintenance (TPM)	• Integration of organisation and systems • Global logistics optimisations (TLS) • System focused on the customer	• Consolidation of process control know-how (reliability techniques, DOE) • Introduction/integration CAD/CAE • Experimental QFD project • Launch of simultaneous engineering	• Quality equals fitness for purpose • Needs for continuous improvement • Internal customer culture
Level 2 (Management by Process)	• Customer satisfaction is the concern of all the organisation • Real-time link with customer and market *"Market in"*	• JIT suppliers • Reduction lead times • Evaluation at total cost • Co-design of project • Self-certification • Improvement by contract • Widespread operational integration	• Priority to process control and total performance • Organisation for the supervision of process capabilities • Total industrial engineering (TIE)	• Integrated logistic process • "Short" chain • Minimum inventories	• Forward engineering • Product QFD extended (positive Q) • Emphasis on start-up times and costs • Time-to-market a priority • Designing process delegated to product teams	• Process culture • Improvement managed by the line • Planning of improvement
Level 3 (Desired state Vision)	• Operating priorities based on real-time customer satisfaction • "Market in" logic in all the processes • Systematic bench-marking of processes performances *"Total Quality"*	• Partnership with principal suppliers • Strategic operated integration • Vendor rating also on strategic assessment • Product/technology co-designed • Integrated logistics network	• Priority to customer satisfaction • Total manu-facturing management (TMM)	• "Short" company (lead time, inventories, operating processes, feedback and management processes)	• Product/process QFD • Compre-hensive approach: quality, start-up time, cost	• "Open company" • "Global" culture

Table 3.2   Company grid example (*cont.*).

Role of management	Management and organisational system	Human resources (role and policies)	Quality activities	Basic methods	Quality system	Information system
• Quality is not a management problem • Responsibility delegated to specific technical functions	• Structure by functions • Functional Taylorist culture • MBO on numerous objectives	• Hierarchy functional relationship • Vertical careers	• Formal respect of the standards • Inspection to specifications • Activities delegated to specialists	• Statistical control techniques • Inspection and certification procedures • Sampling plans (AQL)	• Prescriptive approach • Formal inspection procedures • External standard • Quality assurance manuals	• System based on administrative procedures • Centralisation of procedures and data processing • Bureaucratic system
• Promotion of improvement • Appearance of "policies" • Visible signs of commitment • Direct involvement in improvement problems	• MBO on few priority objectives • First process performance indicators • Management decentralisation • Introduction of policy deployment and process management	• Development of inter-functional professional skills • Focus on the customer and on improvement • Management climate evolution	• Quality improvement through the involvement of all • Training for TQC • Training in problem solving • Collection of data on non-quality costs • Vendor–vendee chain improvements	• SPC techniques • Problem solving • Problem finding • CEDAC diagram • FMEA • Design review • Policy deployment • DRW	• Procedures for managing improvement • Development of quality system: planning (assurance); prevention (control); inspection	• Decentralisation of procedures and processing • TP generalised • Monitoring satisfaction users/customers • Introduction of internal performance indicators • Definition of new management reporting system in MPB logic
• Definition of annual policies • Supervision of priority objectives/processes • Management by process performance indicators	• Increase in delegation • New role of the staff (counselling–support) • Generalised policy deployment process and management • Manager/professional roles	• Process culture • Development of reward system • Development of entre-preneurial capacity of middle managers	• Policy deployment • Analysis needs of internal/external customers and satisfaction monitoring • Management by processes • "Positive" quality designing processes	• Management by processes • Management by policies • Bench-marking • CEDAC system	• Quality equals prevention in the processes • TQC plan and reports • Reduction of inspection costs • QA manual agreed by all and integrated into TQM • Free pass with comakers	• Bench-marking on quality system • Co-definition system architecture • Information system for monitoring and managing processes
• Promotion and support of the "market in"/ "internal customer" logic • Management by policies	• Management by policies and by processes	• Maximum use of cultural and individual energies • "Comprehensive approaches"	• PD and DRW integrated and systematic • Real-time customer satisfaction monitoring with direct feedback • Measurement quality of the system	• Analysis by global costs • Advanced statistical techniques • TQC management system • MBP audit techniques	• Management audits of productivity and quality • Fast feedback from the market • Integrated QA system (suppliers–company) • Complete incoming free pass	• Integration of internal/external EDP system • Real-time monitoring of quality and customer/user satisfaction

approach, a firm has at its disposal an instrument which allows it to plan and manage all its organisational and technical changes coherently. In large firms organised by divisions or grouped together under a holding company, the grid is also a useful tool for assessment which can be used both by the corporate functions and by the operating units to assess their degree of maturity compared to their own reference model.

ORGANISATIONAL SELF-ASSESSMENT

The objective of the self-assessment feature of the global strategic planning model is to identify the main critical issues of the business, projected into a scenario covering a three- to five-year planning horizon. It concerns those critical performance issues which can make the firm lose out to the competition or raise serious doubts over its profitability (occasionally even its survival). These critical issues are expressed as factors or business processes. Examples would be: new product development time, technology, production flexibility, quality, product cost. An analysis of this kind is very important if we are to identify the priorities for strategic or organisational development to be pursued in the plan.

So far as the medium- to long-term competitive factors are concerned, as well as "business factors" (quality costs, market share, etc.), self-assessment should particularly aim to identify the weakest business process, (for example, the new product development process, manufacturing, supply/restocking, distribution, debt collection, etc). In this way it can become the main source for identifying *medium-term priority objectives*, which are usually concerned with organisational issues.

Factors such as costs, revenues, market shares should, of course, already be included in the traditional strategic and business plans. In any case, the self-assessment includes analyses on two fronts: internal and external (customer survey). The analysis of competition, at least of its performance in the marketplace, should also be included in the strategic plan and carried out using a suitable benchmarking process.

- *Internal self-assessment*. There are several ways of carrying this out, each with its own well-defined, standardised methods. The most global approach is the one which simultaneously considers the business processes and the company key business factors. It is advisable to involve the first two levels of operating management in the self-assessment through a "guided" process. The output of the self-assessment should be the identification of the four to six processes and the two or three most critical or important key factors.*

- *The customer survey.* This survey has the objective of identifying which product and service features the customers consider most important, and also current levels of satisfaction (compared with the competition). This enables a "market-in" reasoning to be applied to the critical appraisal of our own organisation and performance, since it helps to identify the critical internal issues to be solved in order to achieve the objective "customer satisfaction". Here again there are standard methods which can be applied to this type of survey.

GLOBAL STRATEGIC PLANNING

Global strategic planning consists of finalising the three basic planning ingredients:

1 The strategic/business plan
2 Self-assessment
3 The grid

into a multi-year plan which is coherent in all its objectives and actions. The *business plan* mainly provides the *short-term* priorities (usually expressed in financial terms or as operating standards) and the financial reference points planned to a timescale ("how much" and "when") including their links with the annual budget. The *self-assessment* provides the *priority medium-term objectives*, mainly in terms of organisation ("where" to act first). The grid with its "policies" provides the inputs for the *long-term objectives* and ensures coherence between the *short-, medium- and long-term actions* (see Table 3.3).

The first time that a comprehensive plan is prepared, its point of departure is, of course, the existing strategic plan (in subsequent years the interaction between the three ingredients takes

---

* G. Merli (1993) *Eurochallenge*, IFS, Bedford

Table 3.3   Synthesis of outputs of the global strategic planning process.

Strategic/business plan	
● Short-term priority objectives	
● Economic and performance references	⇒ "What and when"
Organisational self-assessment	
● Medium-term priority objectives	
(critical issues/competitive advantages)	
● Key factors	⇒ "Where"
● Priority business processes	
(organisational breakthroughs)	
Reference model ("grid")	
● Long-term objectives	
● Reference policies	⇒ "How"
● Logical–temporal sequences	

place first). The traditional strategic plan is usually the company "figures" plan. Normally it simply contains the description of the performance levels planned in quantitative terms. The most common indicators concern the market (shares and absolute volumes), product (volume per product, new products), financial data in general (revenues, costs, investments, financial charges, etc.) and productivity.

These contents are, of course, necessary, even fundamental, but it would be a good thing if the strategic plan included them in a more "aggregated" way for the following years. It is possible to add specific annnual figures if necessary. From an effective planning viewpoint the strategic plan should, however, clearly identify the breakthrough objectives for the first year. For example, this means that for the first year, instead of only planning generalised improvements, say, of 5–10%, in a "breakthrough management" logic it should also include decidedly greater "concentrated" improvements (see the examples of breakthrough objectives).

The global strategic plan aims to plan three other aspects:

1   How to ensure that the "figures" of the strategic plan are adequately pursued through operating plans which translate expectations into a series of objectives and actions which are coherent in the short, medium and long term (through correct policy deployment)

2 The changes which must be made in order to ensure the continuous strengthening of the competitiveness of the business. This includes planning development in:
- The organisational system
- The business culture
- Methodological and technical capabilities

The output of a global planning process is a multi-year plan based on groups of objectives of both the types described, qualitative and organisational–cultural, "packaged by year" (see Figure 3.6).

The "qualitative objectives" column in Figure 3.6 contains the objectives planned in the strategic plan, while the organisational/technical objectives column ("other objectives") contains the objectives which are necessary to achieve its numerical targets and, in particular, what is required to strengthen the competitiveness of the business organisation over the medium and long term (this can be the Total Quality Plan if it has already been launched in the organisation).

The following is an example of coherence between a figures and an organisational objective: if the strategic plan anticipates a 10% increase in the outputs produced by the plants, the organisational objectives columns should plan for the same year (or probably already in the previous year) a major Total Productive Maintenance or Statistical Process Control (SPC) programme. If this is not provided for, the left-hand (figures) column risks becoming a "wish-list" whose vanity will later become apparent to all.

An example of a long-term organisational objective would be to "develop the capacity to reduce time to market, in order to maintain competitiveness in terms of products suitable to the market and to competition". The plan will then in the right-hand columns make provision for organisational change programmes such as *simultaneous engineering*. It may be noted that the medium- to long-term organisational and cultural objectives are derived directly from the boxes in the grid (they are the objectives linked to the reference patterns foreseen for the future) and from the outputs of self-assessment.

An example of a global objectives plan is given in Figure 3.7. In its structure it is very similar to what is used by Xerox where

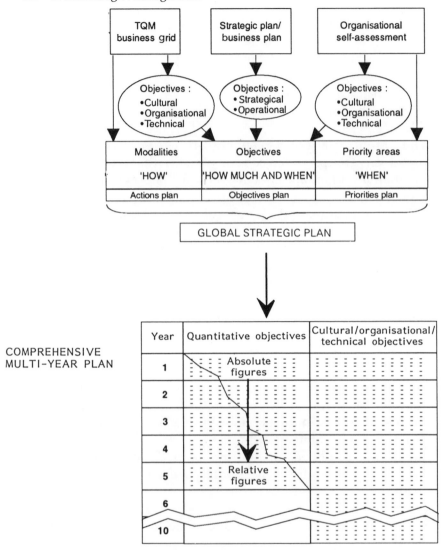

Figure 3.6   *Global strategic planning.*

precisely this parallel deployment of *what* and *how* exists. The global strategic plan is, of course, a *rolling* plan updated annually.

The planning horizons should cover at least seven to ten years for the organisational and cultural objectives (organisational and cultural capabilities cannot be improvised), and less than five

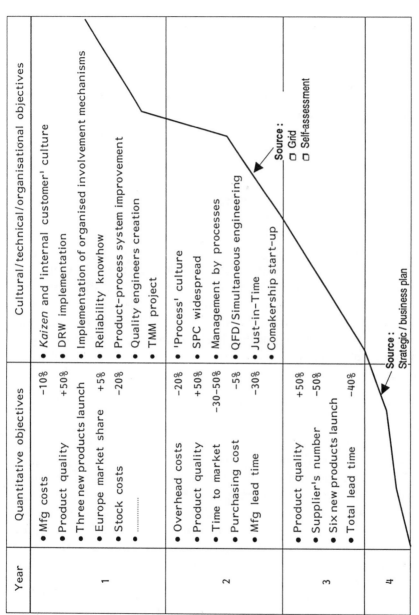

Year	Quantitative objectives	Cultural/technical/organisational objectives
1	• Mfg costs −10% • Product quality +50% • Three new products launch • Europe market share +5% • Stock costs −20% •	• *Kaizen* and 'internal customer' culture • DRW implementation • Implementation of organised involvement mechanisms • Reliability knowhow • Product-process system improvement • Quality engineers creation • TMM project
2	• Overhead costs −20% • Product quality +50% • Time to market −30–50% • Purchasing cost −5% • Mfg lead time −30%	• 'Process' culture • SPC widespread • Management by processes • QFD/Simultaneous engineering • Just-in-Time • Comakership start-up
3	• Product quality +50% • Supplier's number −50% • Six new products launch • Total lead time −40%	
4		

Source :
Strategic / business plan

Source :
◻ Grid
◻ Self-assessment

Figure 3.7 *A comprehensive strategic plan.*

years for the figures objectives (today it is already difficult to make credible projections for more than three years). For these objectives the indicators will, however, give precise, absolute values for the first year, "softening" them progressively until they are only relative data (compared with competition and the financial scenario) for the final projections.

This pattern of a strategic plan is obviously phased on the following entrepreneurial reasoning:

- "The success of the business depends above all on long-term strategic and organisational choices which cannot be supported by figures"
- "In the strategic plan the figures are simply the operational confirmation of long-term entrepreneurial choices"

With this reasoning it is easy to understand why in these strategic plans the organisational and cultural developments are planned over ten-year horizons, whereas figures only appear up to the fifth year or even less. This is the opposite of the traditional approach, which is usually to define organisational and cultural developments on the basis of short- and medium-term financial objectives.

PREPARING THE ANNUAL PLAN

The annual plan is, of course, inspired by the global strategic plan, but it is laid out in terms of measurements and priorities for the year, taking account of the current scenario and the main problems experienced during the previous period ("absolute" problems or obstacles met in carrying out the previous annual plan). The reference process is set out in Figure 3.8. The point of departure suggested is the analysis of the main existing problems (the operating priorities) which are then confronted with the short- and medium-term priorities. (It is also the approach used by the Japanese in *Hoshin Kanri*).

The effective aproach, as we have seen, requires the choice of only a small number of priorities each year, in order to ensure a high level of effectiveness in terms of business impact. The priorities, expressed as short- and medium-term objectives, should

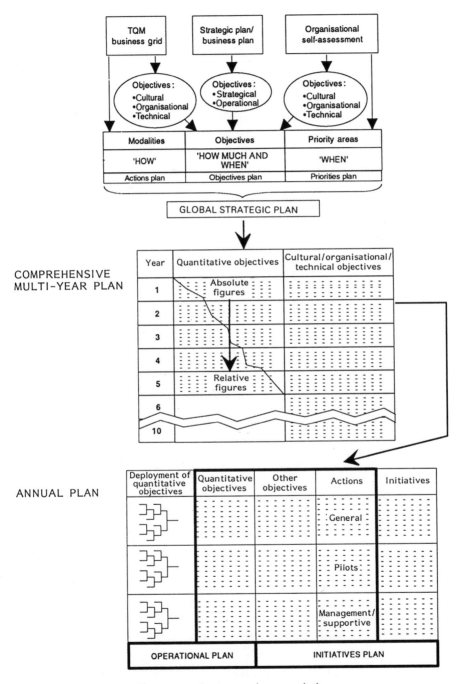

Figure 3.8 *Setting up the annual plan.*

be chosen using the criteria described above. The best output is one which defines the general policy guidelines and the two operating priorities for the year (as described above). The two priorities should therefore be:

1   The priority short-term objective (problems to be resolved or results to be pursued; normally with reference to economic/ quantitative performance)
2   The priority medium-term objective (difficulties to be eliminated or competitive advantage to be pursued; normally refers to a business process performance or an organisational capability)

The types of objective in question can be found in Table 3.1. The ideal situation is one where the short- and medium-term priorities both require action in the same areas or on the same processes or factors (for example, production, lead time or costs). In this case, by concentrating on few areas, but with actions which make their impact at different points in time, we can achieve the highest possible level of effectiveness and coherence. In fact:

- Focusing on a limited area makes the result highly effective.
- Facing up at the same time to issues which have an impact on different time horizons makes it easier to check the coherence of the actions planned and to take advantage of synergy.
- Attacking a difficulty to transform it into a competitive advantage generates a highly motivating, challenging situation and avoids dispersion of effort.

A typical situation is one in which these priority objectives break down at the first level of deployment into one to three "figures" objectives and two to four "other" objectives (see the example in Figure 3.9). For the one to three "figures" objectives the logic of breakthrough management requires major improvement to be programmed (as we have already seen, at least 30% of existing theoretical improvement margins). These objectives need a specific plan and *special management*. It is on this plan that we suggest that the breakthrough management process described in the following chapters should be focused.

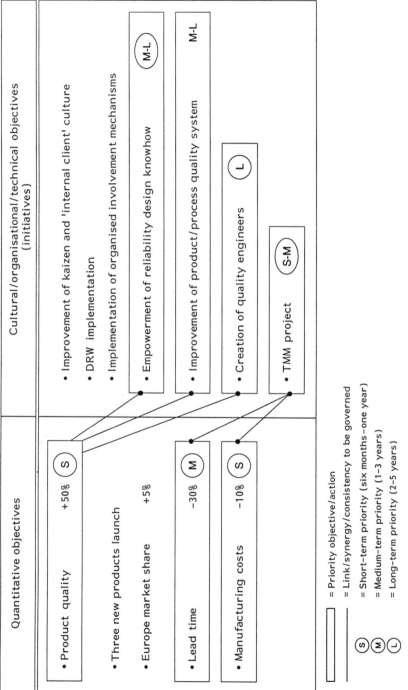

Figure 3.9 *An example of an annual plan with priority objectives.*

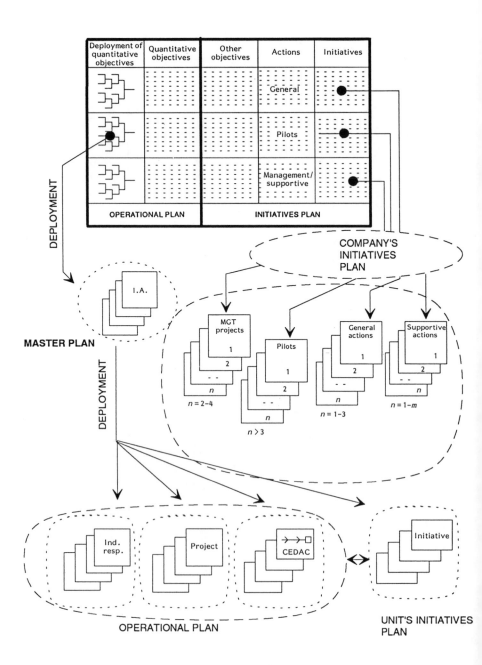

Figure 3.10   *An annual plan.*

The "tree explosion" of three objectives set out on the left of the global strategic plan in Figure 3.8 illustrates precisely this concept of choosing priorities. This "explosion" is the basis of the operating plan (see Figure 3.10) which targets the pursuit of the priority objectives for the year. For the remaining "figures" objectives where it will content itself with 3–5% annual improvements, the firm will rely on its normal mechanism (Total Quality if this has been introduced), delegating responsibility to the organisation, and control to the normal process of budgeting and management reporting. For the actions and initiatives required to achieve the "other" objectives, we need, on the other hand, to conceive what we can call an "initiatives plan". This plan concerns the operating capacities of the company which must be developed during the year. Checking the coherence of the figures objectives with the other objectives, and therefore between the operating plan, and the initiatives plan, is a basic feature of annual planning. The logic behind the checking and management of the coherence between the operating plan and the initiatives plan is illustrated in Figures 3.9 and 3.10.

The initiatives plan (also called the Total Quality plan) normally takes into account four types of action:

1 General actions
2 Pilot areas
3 Top management projects
4 Supporting actions

They can be defined as follows:

1 *General actions:* initiatives necessary to implement what has been laid down in the grid at company level. They concern large-scale activities affecting most or all of the organisation. An example would be the implementation of a "supplier–customer" programme throughout the firm (Daily Routine Work—DRW project).
2 *Top management projects:* initiatives directly involving top management. For example:
   • Priority business projects of a strategic nature (for example, setting up a comakership project with suppliers)
   • Revision of the management reward system

- Symbolic projects (e.g. "debureaucratisation")
3 *Pilot areas:* activated for a variety of reason, such as:
   - To demonstrate the effectiveness of new approaches (in this case the objectives will be limited in coverage, but important)
   - To experiment with and personalise methodologies which it is intended to extend in future years (e.g. SEDAC, Policy Deployment, Process Management)
4 *Supporting actions:* initiatives to ensure the success of the plan through coherent changes in:
   - Company organisation
   - Management system
   - Performance appraisal
   - Information system
   - Industrial relations
   - Total Quality organisation
   - etc

THE SPECIAL MANAGEMENT OF PRIORITIES

The bridge between "effective planning" and "effective operating management" *is the operating plan for the special management of priorities*, which enables us:

- To have a specific programme of responsibilities and actions focused on the priority objectives (not diluted by a plethora of budget data)
- To identify indicators for day-to-day management (and not only *post hoc* accounting data)
- To assign ambitious, challenging objectives, freed from the dangerous logic that "the objective = budgeted performance"
- To allow line management to participate directly in the planning, management and control of the priority objectives of the business

Although this plan is concerned only with a small number of important objectives, it is clear that it must be coherent with the normal management plan contained in the budget. The relationship between this special management plan and the budget is

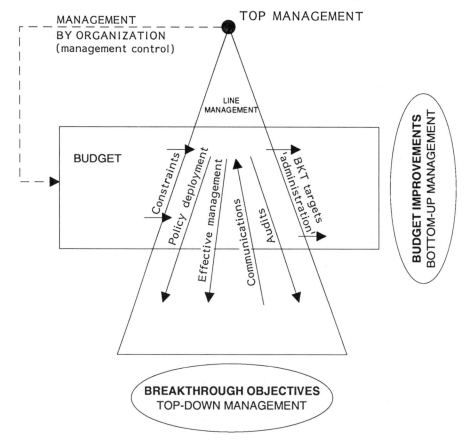

Figure 3.11 *Special management and budgeting.*

illustrated in Figure 3.11. The criteria governing this relationship can be described as follows:

1 The objectives contained in the special management plan are usually more ambitious than those of the budget. The budget must be the plan containing the level of performance which the firm is most likely to achieve during the year, so that reference standards can be extracted. To ensure that a sufficiently ambitious budget is achieved, some of the actual results must be better than budget (preferably those related to priority objectives) to compensate for those which, for a variety of reasons, will fall below standard. There is only one exception to this criterion: when the company is fighting for

survival. In this case it can even happen that very ambitious breakthrough objectives have to be set as part of the budget.

2   The budget treats all the objectives (priority or not) in the same way with the same level of breakdown for all. It normally applies deployment by function and staff position down to a predefined responsibility level (the cost centre).

3   The supervision of the performance taken into account by the budget is carried out by the company organisation using the mechanism and procedures of management reporting, at predefined frequencies (usually monthly).

4   The indicators used in the budget usually measure past performance by the use of accounting data (from the analytical cost accounting system).

5   The indicators used in special management are chosen by the managers and supervisors who are concerned with the breakthrough objectives, as the best possible operating indicators for measuring improvements in the processes which are to generate the desired results (usually "process" indicators, that is, causal factors and not output).

6   The relationship between the special management operating indicators and the budget indicators can be mathematical or simply by correlation. Eventually "bridges" can be built between the two types of indicators to assess the effect on the final result, when the process result is well ahead in time (for example, for objectives concerning organisational capabilities such as lead time or flexibility).

7   The supervision and management of the "special management" indicators is a direct task of the line, starting with the manager responsible for the planned result. The control mechanisms are also special, and the frequency of control is not defined in advance (but to be effective it should be daily, or at least weekly).

8   The budget takes into account all the economic side of the breakthrough objectives coordinated by special management:

   ● It contains all forecast costs (which become expenditure or investment limits for the special management plan)
   ● It includes (as mentioned earlier) part of the anticipated financial results
   ● It identifies other eventual constraints

SUMMARY

Breakthrough management must begin with the "effective planning" of the business objectives. The first step in an effective planning process is to identify the priority objectives. These are chosen bearing in mind that for the business they must ensure:

- The short-term economic results
- Its competitive capabilities over the medium and long term
- Its operating coherence

The mix between actions with short-term impact (e.g. cost reduction) and medium-term impact (e.g. reductions in lead time or time to market) must be managed carefully but also "entrepreneurially". The objectives must necessarily be limited in number (the law of priorities), coherent (through the use of "policies"), clearly defined, and manageable (introduction of suitable operating indicators). The references used for preparing the strategic plan must therefore contain the elements necessary to meet these requirements.

This approach to strategic planning is called "global strategic planning", since it contains the ingredients required to ensure the global coverage of all the objectives of the plan. The ingredients used are:

- *The traditional strategic plan* which provides the strategic objectives (if it does not exist, it is sufficient to define the priorities in terms of the operating results which one wants to obtain over time)
- *Organisational self-assessment* which helps to identify the organisational improvement priorities which will be necessary to ensure the competitiveness of the business in future years
- *The reference model (the grid)* which provides the policy guidelines for steering the development of the business towards its vision and for ensuring that the actions planned are coherent with each other

The global strategic plan constitutes the main reference point from which to define the annual plan. The other reference, which is also the prime input to the preparation of the annual plan, is the analysis of the present scenario and the main operating problems encountered during the previous period.

To ensure that management is effective, the annual plan must highlight the "priorities of the year" (the "red" objectives). It is on these that the real "breakthrough management" plan is constructed, i.e. the plan for the special management of breakthrough objectives. To make this plan coherent with the company budget, some particular points require attention. One general principle is to make provision for "special plan" objectives more ambitious than those included in the budget (which, by definition, should contain performance projections and not challenging objectives).

4
Effectiveness in Operating Management

INTRODUCTION

In Chapter 3 we saw how to identify and plan priority objectives. We also introduced the concept of the "special management" of these objectives, and gave particular attention to its links with the planning process and the budget. In this chapter we shall get to the heart of the subject of special management, and we shall describe a number of ways of ensuring effectiveness in the operating management of breakthrough objectives, that is, in the process of *converting objectives into results*.

We shall suggest an operating organisation based on approaches and tools which are a combination and a simplification of international best practice. In particular, we shall describe an approach which derives its management philosophy from Japanese Management by Policy, and its behavioural approach from the successful entrepreneurs of small and medium-sized European firms. The whole is "seasoned" with visual management tools developed by Ryuji Fukuda (Deming prizewinner for this work) and by Galgano & Associates. This methodology has now been adopted by several dozen large and medium-sized firms including most of those quoted in Chapter 1.

THE EFFECTIVE MANAGEMENT PROCESS

The *effective operating management* process is characterized by the following requirements:

1   To be capable of identifying priority operating objectives
2   To be capable of assigning the right responsibilities
3   To be capable of identifying the most appropriate operating indicators and targets
4   To be capable of managing priorities "in real time" (day by day)
5   To be capable of "visual supervision" of the indicators of the priority objectives
6   To be capable of spotting the current bottlenecks blocking the priority objectives
7   To be capable of dealing effectively with the bottlenecks

These requirements bring to life the basic principle ("the entrepreneur's dream") of breakthrough management, which is that "the main task of a manager at each level is to work every day on the priority business objectives, and to concentrate on removing the bottlenecks in the process on which their achievement depends". It is in fact obvious that time spent on other objectives or on the first problem which we may encounter would be less productive. Let us then see how it is possible to satisfy these "seven requirements of breakthrough management" through an operating process.

The problem of identifying priority objectives has been dealt with in Chapter 3, while the criteria for effective management were discussed in Chapter 2. It now remains to describe the operating process which allows the other requirements to be met.

The overall design of the process is illustrated in Figure 4.1. It makes ample use of the visual management tools of the Ryuji Fukuda SEDAC system. This set of tools supports all of breakthrough management starting from the second requirement listed above, but is particularly effective compared with current methodologies from the fourth requirement onwards (the capability to manage priorities in "real time").

The management approach proposed is based exclusively on operating indicators as opposed to traditional management

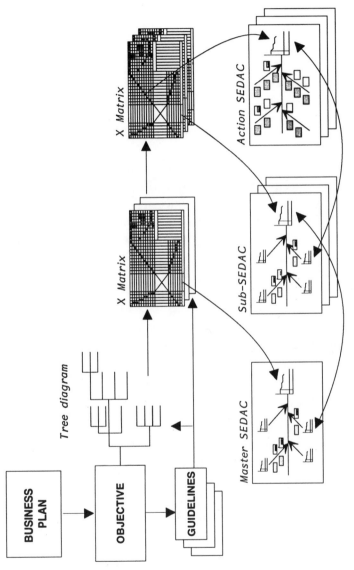

Figure 4.1 The effective management cycle.

reporting focused on results. Its operating process is based on the use of four sequential phases which make up the *breakthrough management cycle* (a simplified version of the PDCA of Management by Policy). The four phases are as follows:

1   Planning and programming
2   Organising management
3   Operating
4   Monitoring and managing

PLANNING AND PROGRAMMING

This phase concerns the identification and planning of the actions required to pursue the breakthrough objectives chosen for *special management*. It usually concerns objectives for the improvement of operating performance. This is because it is only possible to speak of "major improvements" of existing activities (otherwise they are innovations or "drastic action"), and also because what is dealt with here only concerns the improvement of what can be measured operationally. By innovation and drastic action we mean actions such as "set up a joint venture" or "close a factory", for which we need to set up a project or assign a specific responsibility rather than ensure effective management.

Returning to the operating objectives, the process which turns a priority objective into a coherent operating action plan is normally called Policy Deployment (*Hoshin Planning*). The term Policy, borrowed from Management by Policy, picks up and highlights all the various elements which should be taken into account in launching actions to achieve an objective. These elements consist of:

- Type of objective (the "direction")
- Indicators and numerical targets
- Reference guidelines
- Constraints and assumptions

These are indispensable to breakthrough management taken in its widest entrepreneurial sense as described in Chapter 2.

Table 4.1 Policy example.

Direction	Target	External conditions	Guidelines
Reduction in purchased material cost	−18% in two years	Quality level of product at least as today	Set-up of a total costs vendor rating system
		Do not change suppliers	Comakership
		Do not increase raw materials stock	Reduction in number of suppliers

Indeed, for this to occur, the prime requirement is for the objective to be clearly identified and defined in terms of satisfactory results (indicators and targets). The second requirement is for the objective to be coherent with the other short- and medium-term objectives (this is ensured by the guidelines or by the policies themselves). The third requirement is for it to be compatible with the resources available and with the economic parameters of the budget, and that it should not prejudice other areas of performance (these are protected by the "constraints and assumptions"). An example of a good definition of an objective in Policy Deployment terms is given in Table 4.1.

Coming now to the meaning of "Deployment", which is more or less synonymous with breakdown or explosion. Policy Deployment is a methodology and a process which permits the "cascade" breakdown of a policy or an objective into:

- Improvement areas
- Operating indicators and targets
- Responsibilities
- Projects/actions
- Resources
- Timescale

The action plan, which has been derived from Policy Deployment, must include everything which is "necessary and sufficient" to obtain the desired result. It is obviously a process which is applied only to the priority objectives and which will also apply to itself the same logic of only choosing operating priorities.

The concept of the Policy Deployment process is illustrated in Figure 4.2. This also shows the logic of deployment "by priority", in the sense that at each level only the priority factors are broken down and included in the special management arrangements. This priority deployment logic, linked to the need to define the policies (the "how") for each of the elements planned, makes it impossible to confuse this process with the usual budgeting planning procedures. This characteristic is absolutely fundamental to effective planning.

The choice of priorities at each deployment level should be tailor-made, and should not simply be a Pareto approach based on the relative importance of the factors considered. The criteria for choosing priorities should not simply be their arithmetic impact on the objective (their relative "weight"), but should be the product of "weight × ease of achievement". This means that we shall seek out the best combination between the weight of the factor and the estimated likelihood of getting results out of it. In Total Quality jargon, we are looking for the best combination of $B \times Q$ (where B = Business, stands for "level of impact on the business" and Q = Quality, for "existing improvement margins").

By "tailor-made", on the other hand, we mean that once the priorities have been identified, we replan the numerical target to be assigned to them. If, for example, the deployment process has initially identified the need to improve five indicators by 5–7% and three by 15–20%, once the priorities have been decided the targets will be redefined, raising the objectives for the priority factors and probably reducing the others. This makes use of the concept that "effectiveness equals concentrating on priorities". Priorities are identified so that special management can be applied to them in order to reach a high level of effectiveness. We shall probably not be able to supervise the other factors with the same attention and effectiveness. This means that we must extract the maximum effectiveness from special management and obtain the most significant results possible.

But "tailor-made" can have an even broader meaning. This is in the unfortunate case where deployment does not highlight any priority factors or objectives (a "flat Pareto" where a large number of factors/objectives appear all with the same order of importance or difficulty). In this case, to arrive at a focused

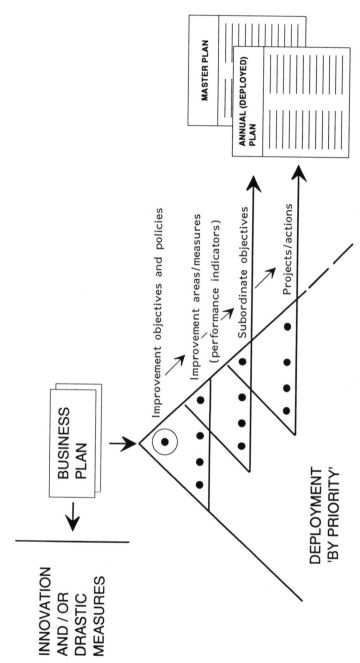

Figure 4.2 *The policy-deployment process.*

entrepreneurial management approach we must "force" the situation and *make ourselves choose some priorities*. In this process some objectives will be emphasised so as to create the more focused situation required for breakthrough management.

It is perhaps worth recalling that the capacity to "manage by priorities" is a basic requirement of entrepreneurial management which is conceptually the opposite of the "optimising" management capacity, based on supervising large numbers of objectives and indicators. It must also be remembered that "entrepreneurial management" is synonymous with the capacities of the human being, whereas "optimising management" is synonymous with management through systems and data management capabilities.

Management based on the supervision of two or three factors rather than ten or twenty is therefore more human and entrepreneurial. In fact it will be easier to achieve improvement of 30% in two or three "manageable" areas than 5–10% in ten to twenty areas which are only "controllable".

The final principle of Policy Deployment for breakthrough management is that it should cascade down to the lowest possible levels, and should identify the elementary actions necessary and the individual operating targets. It is very likely that at this level we are including foremen, employees and workers. At the same time, we shall probably not need to involve some of the managers even at senior levels since deployment, rather than seeking to satisfy aesthetic or hierarchical criteria, is strictly searching out those actions and those responsibilities, wherever they may be, which can really contribute to the achievement of the priority objectives.

The priority elements identified through the deployment process will be called *red objectives/indicators/factors*, i.e. those generated by business priorities. Staff not directly involved in the management of the "red" objectives of a management cycle are normally used as support staff. They are, however, mainly concerned with the management of other "green" objectives derived from "local" priorities which they themselves have identified (also using the "cascade" approach applied to their own area). What is certain is that a "green" objective can never block a "red" one, even if the person responsible for the green objective has a higher grade than the one responsible for the red one with which he or she could interfere (with the result or with the use of resources).

This concept can potentially have an even stronger impact, and offer an even greater opportunity for improving the management of the business (although it is equally true that it can represent a problem for very functional/hierarchical cultures). The basic management criterion involved is that "in the operations of a business it is the objective that must be in command, not the hierarchy". This means that the management mechanisms must allow for moments/projects/actions where, depending on the skills required, persons of a lower grade may have to manage the contribution of people of a higher grade than themselves. Without entering into its possible organisational implications (to be seen as opportunities rather than a necessity) let us simply accept this principle for the purposes of special management and therefore by exception. We shall certainly be more effective.

Returning to the Policy Deployment process, it must be stressed that this is not carried out by programmes, or by the managers by themselves as a desk exercise. It requires each level of deployment to be agreed with the persons concerned. For each level of deployment three hierarchic levels are normally in fact involved (but levels in terms of objectives and not of position). It should, moreover, be noted that today in a "lean" company, even if it is very large, there should not be more than three levels in its organisation concerned with Operations. The involvement of three levels is a direct consequence of the planning procedure. Each level is involved with the level above in receiving inputs regarding policies and targets.

It is then involved with the level below for the same reasons, and returns to the higher level in order to readjust the first hypothesis (in Management by Policy this approach is called *catch ball*).

The whole is an iterative process which can go through a number of cycles. The result of this procedure will be a plan accepted at all levels, including agreement on its targets, the means for pursuing them, and particularly on the indicators to be managed.

It is worth observing that the contents of a plan developed by the use of Policy Deployment are also different from the contents of a traditional budget. In fact it is not so much a deployment of objectives as a deployment of the actions necessary to achieve the objectives. That is because the objective of an "effective plan" is not to build a reference for management reporting but to provide line management with the operating indicators and targets which they require to achieve the planned results.

A really good deployment will therefore, at each level in the breakdown, take two steps which are fundamental to breakthrough management:

1   From the general to the particular
2   From the effect to the cause

"From the general to the particular" means that deployment must succeed in identifying all the sub-priorities through which the desired overall result can be obtained. "From the effect to the cause" means that to be effective, deployment must at each stage identify the priority causal factors to be tackled in order to obtain the result.

The Japanese call this process *upper stream control*, and the corresponding system as "management by process/cause" instead of "by results". A criticism frequently levelled at our breakthrough plans by Japanese managers is that they often look little different from our budgets (with more or less detail). They appear more useful for management reporting or control than for operating management. Very often they simply set out the deployment of the objectives into sub-objectives in the form of results and subsidiary results expected, rather than the improvements which must be made upstream to the causes of the improved results. This is probably another key step: to understand that *to be effective in improving results, we must, above all, know how to identify the principal "levers" for obtaining them*, that is, the variables in the processes upstream on which the results depend.

For example, if the objective is to improve the quality of a product by 50%, the first deployment level (management, not budgetary) must consist of identifying the main cause of defects (e.g. assembly and machining) and not simply the types of defect; the second level must identify the underlying causes (e.g.

heat treatment and work cycles) and the third level, causes even further upstream (e.g. the process capabilities of the oven temperature and deficiencies in the work cycle descriptions), etc. (Figure 4.3).

In this way we shall be able to work out a plan which, by setting up a breakthrough in the process capability of oven temperature and in the preparation of the assembly cycles, will make it possible to obtain a corresponding breakthrough improvement in the quality of the final product. The alternative would have been to rely on a plan broken down into a number of 50% improvements which when added up might (possibly) have produced a similar improvement in output, but which would have involved a much bigger, more burdensome operation to manage.

The management priorities which in this case can already guarantee 80% or more of the final result were identified as "oven temperature process capability" and "number of cycle lines not defined". Breakthrough operating management will therefore focus on these in order to obtain rapid results. It is as if we had identified the *"critical path"* towards the objective and avoided fragmenting our efforts ineffectively on everything. In reality the example is deliberately over-simplified, since at the lowest level of deployment there are usually more than two priorities (although this can happen when a few bottlenecks are the real problem). The remaining 10–20% of the result will be picked up though normal local "bottom-up" or "campaign" improvement management, without tight supervision or special management arrangements.

Returning to the Policy Deployment process, it is also useful to think of the *time* dimension. How long should a Policy Deployment cycle last, that is, the time taken to make a breakthrough objectives plan? It should take between one week and two months. Why such a wide span of time? It is because the time taken (and the validity of the plan) depends on many factors, in particular the level of knowledge of cause-and-effect relationships inside the firm. It is not by accident that the Japanese claim that today they are capable of good deployment because they have invested thirty years of research into cause-and-effect relationships! The time taken will be very short if there is a detailed knowledge of these relationships, and very

80

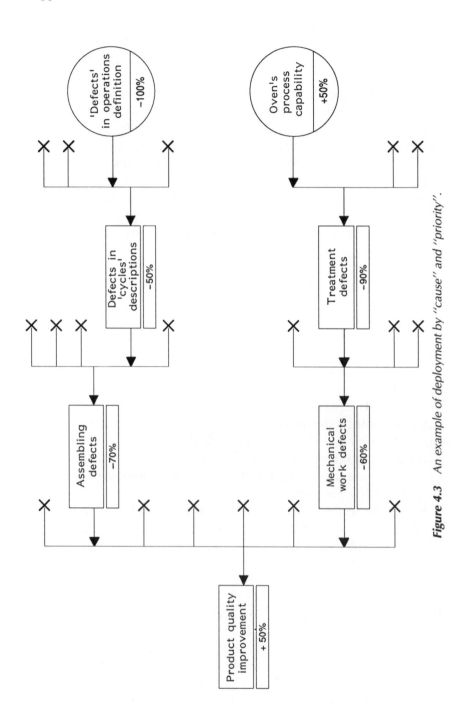

Figure 4.3 An example of deployment by "cause" and "priority".

long if not enough is known and research and analysis of historical data are necessary. But the time will also be very short if almost nothing is known, as in that case without completely abandoning effective planning it will be necessary to use a very different interactive or iterative process, and afterwards refine it through a series of more detailed phases.

This first deployment will then simply consist of indicators representing the results that we want to achieve. It is impossible to do anything else if we do not have enough information to identify the "leverage" or causal factors. Deployment will be very fast, needing only qualitative and arithmetical expressions.

This first deployment, although it already aims at achieving some results, will mainly be used to search out the causes, the levers to be used to obtain the results and therefore the indicators for the upstream variables among which we must look for priorities (in this case the "Plan" of PDCA will be partly in progress at the same time as "Check" and "Act").

SEDAC cascade diagram applications (see below) are very useful in this situation. These are in fact tools designed for the interactive supervision of the phases Plan, Do, Check, and Act at the same time, but they are also useful for the phase in which the real causes of a problem or of obstacles in the way of an objective are studied.

The outcome of this initial research will allow us to move progressively towards a more informed and focused deployment (using "better" cause-and-effect flows).

Returning to the simplified process methodologies suggested, the best tool for effective deployment is the *tree diagram*, one of the seven management tools developed by the Japanese (the other six are the Affinity Diagram—useful for refining vague objectives—the Relationships Diagram, the Matrix Diagram, the Arrow Diagram, the Matrix-Data Analysis and the Decision Tree. Figure 4.4 illustrates the use of the tree diagram.

Its use in the reference framework proposed is shown in Figure 4.5. We suggest that the following criteria should be applied when it is used in breakthrough management:

- Identify the priorities at each level of deployment, based on data, cause-and-effect analyses and on "entrepreneurial" choices (subjective evaluations)

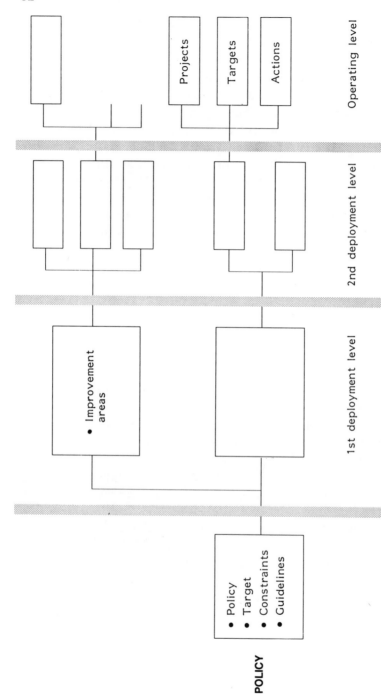

Figure 4.4 "Tree" deployment.

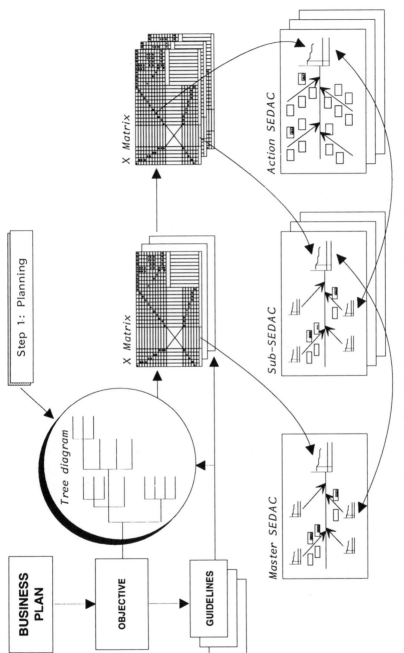

Figure 4.5 The effective management cycle: planning.

- Describe them using the most appropriate management indicators (cause/upstream variables)
- On the priority "branches", complete the deployment down to the operating level (projects, operating actions to be launched)
- Interrupt the deployment on the non-priority branches
- Obtain consensus at each deployment level (involving the levels above and below)

Two examples following these criteria are shown in Figures 4.6 and 4.7.

The results of the planning phase carried out using the Policy Deployment process should therefore be presented in "tree" form. It represents what we want to achieve, and is the starting point for setting up the management arrangements. In Figure 4.8 we give the tree diagram which will be used as a case for developing the remaining phases.

ORGANISING MANAGEMENT

Objectives and Approach

Once we have defined the priorities, the indicators and the targets at each deployment level using the tree diagram, we can then move on to the phase of *organising their management*. In terms of methodological content this is the heaviest phase of the process. It is also the most important event in special management, since its output defines where it is possible to apply the real-time visual management approach which we have already said is fundamental to operating effectiveness.

In graphic terms this phase is concerned with preparing the part of Figure 4.9 marked as Phase 2. It can be considered as the bridge between *planning and operating*. The objective of the organising management phase is *to create an effective link between planning and operating management* through:

1 "Mapping out" the organisation required to pursue the objective
2 Setting up the visual supervision of the entire operating management process related to it

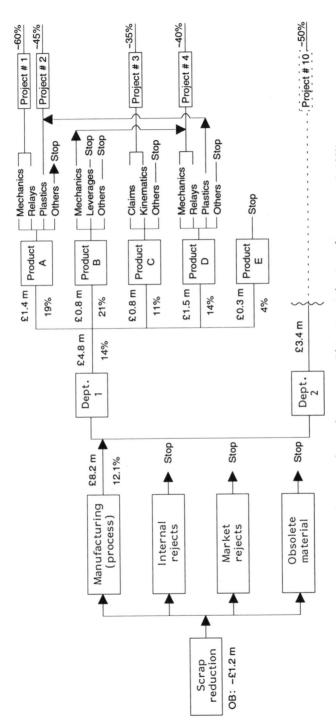

Figure 4.6 *An electromechanical company. Objective: reduction of scrap costs (−40%).*

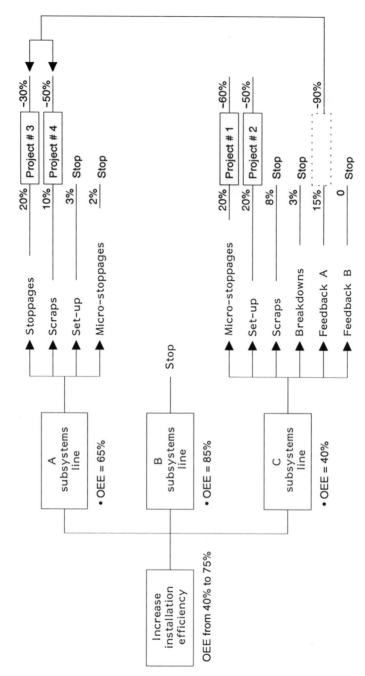

Figure 4.7 *A mechanical company. Objective: increase overall equipment efficiency (OEE from 40% to 75%).*

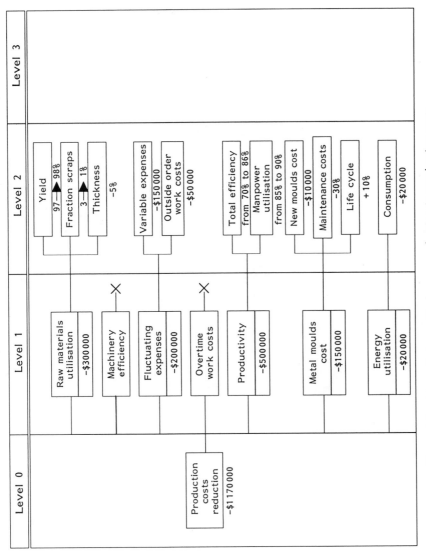

Figure 4.8 A tree diagram. Study case: reduction in production costs.

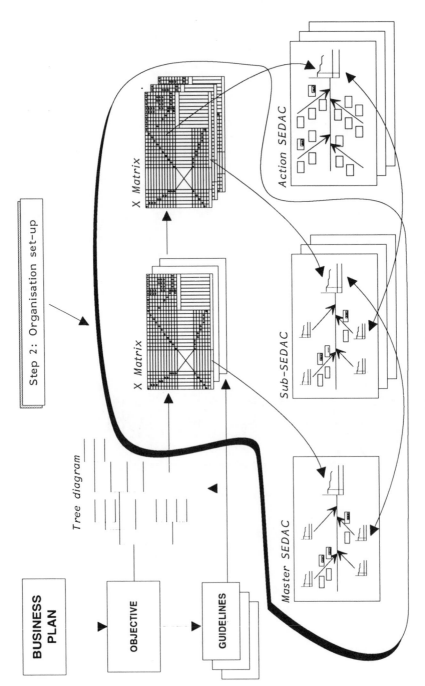

Figure 4.9 The effective management cycles: organisation set-up.

The instrument recommended for mapping is the *Policy/Objective Matrix*, usually called the P/O Matrix or the X Matrix after its shape. The methodology proposed for setting up visual supervision is the SEDAC System and, in particular, Master and Sub-SEDAC.

The X Matrix

The X Matrix contains the following information:

- A summary of the ways in which we intend to pursue the objective and, in particular, the operating targets selected
- The assignment of responsibilities for the indicator targets
- The policy guidelines associated with the various projects/actions
- The organisation planned for pursuing the targets
- The timetable for the project/actions

The first point covers the summaries of what has been planned in the tree diagrams at each level. This means that there will be a tree diagram for each homogeneous group of objectives, that is, for each explosion of a branch of the tree diagram and at each level. See the example of a first-level X Matrix in Figure 4.10, developed from the example given in the previous paragraph.

From a first-level X Matrix there can then be three to five second-level X Matrices and six to ten, if necessary, at the third level. The number of matrices required depends on the degree of breakdown of the tree diagram which is their prime source of data. A complete deployment process is therefore summarised in a cascade of X Matrices (Figure 4.11). The synthesis of the ways in which the objective is to be pursued (improvement areas, indicators, targets) is derived from the tree diagram.

The type of information and data included in the X Matrices will depend on the deployment level to which they refer and the "business maturity" of the firm in terms of breakthrough management/Management by Policy. For a first-level matrix it may be sufficient to include the following data:

- General objective
- Improvement areas

- Indicators
- Targets
- Responsibilities
- Quantitative breakdown of the objective by improvement area

The X Matrix given as an example in Figure 4.10 is limited to these factors. It shows the general objective in zone A, the improvement areas in zone B, the indicators in zone C, the targets in zone D, the quantitative breakdown in zone E and the responsibilities in zone F. The open circles represent the graphic links between the elements in the matrix. In zone F the solid circles represent "prime responsibilities" compared with the co-responsibilities represented by the open circles.

We will now see how to prepare a first-level X Matrix. Let us take Figure 4.12 as a reference and compare it step by step with Figure 4.10. The entry point is zone A, where we insert the total quantitative value of the objective to be pursued. This can be a money value, time (for an objective to reduce lead time), a percentage (for example, the improvement of a qualitative parameter), etc. In our example it is the amount to be saved, i.e. $1 170 000.

Next we fill in zone B, where we put the first-level improvement area indicated in the tree diagram deployment (i.e. the priority areas selected). In our case they are Raw material cost, Fluctuating expenses, Labour cost, Moulds cost, Power consumption.

In zone C we then fill in the indicators chosen. In our example in the improvement area Raw Material, the indicators are "Yield", "Scrap", "Thickness losses". These are linked graphically to the improvement area to which they refer by circles (or crosses).

In zone D we put the reference target (result to be obtained) for each indicator, perhaps expressed in terms of "present situation" and "objective" (from . . . to . . .). We then insert in zone E the values corresponding to the target in terms of their contribution to the general objective, and check the coherence between the two.

In our example we have inserted each of the financial contributions to the total savings planned. It can be seen that so far, we have transferred to the X Matrix only the elements which were

91

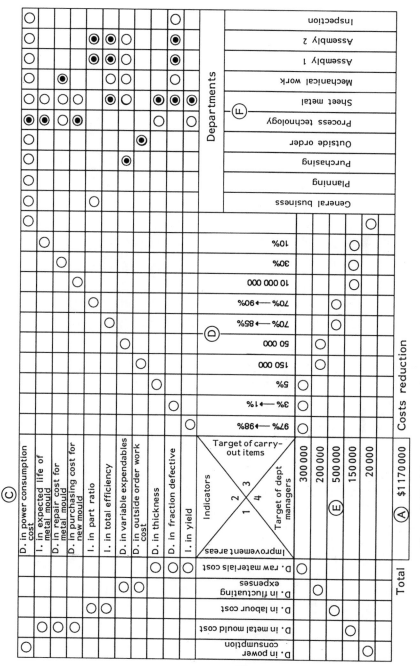

Figure 4.10 The X Matrix. Study case: reduction in manufacturing costs.

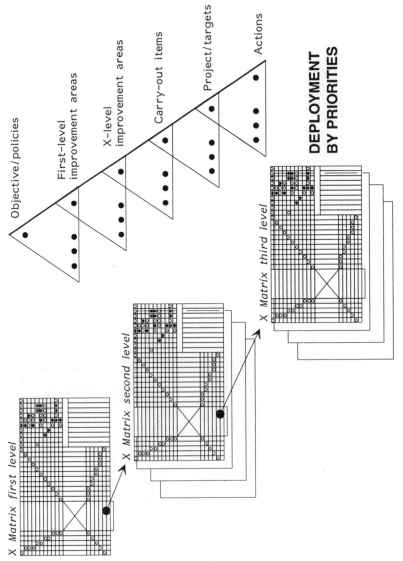

Objective/policies

First-level
improvement areas

X-level
improvement areas

Carry-out items

Project/targets

Actions

**DEPLOYMENT
BY PRIORITIES**

X Matrix first level

X Matrix second level

X Matrix third level

Figure 4.11   Deployment by the X Matrix.

already defined through the tree diagram. The X matrix is useful to check that we have broken the target down sufficiently, and to identify any incoherent elements or the absence (or duplication) of any steps in the logic chain. The X Matrix is also a very compact document, easy to understand thanks to its graphic form.

However, its real added value compared with the tree diagram starts to appear when we begin to prepare zone E which concerns responsibilities. It is at this point that we must define the people to whom we assign responsibility for operating results. They are obviously the people who were involved in identifying the ways chosen for tackling the objective. In the first stage of the process of organising management, these responsibilities mainly concern carrying out the next level of deployment. Once the whole iterative deployment process has been completed, they can be confirmed or, if necessary, changed.

The "definitive" responsibilities are usually identified at three levels:

1 *Direct or prime responsibility* (represented by a solid circle). This is the assignment of full responsibility and leadership for the objective. The selection is made much more on the basis of competence than of the level and status of the persons concerned.
2 *Co-responsibility* (represented by an open circle). The "co-responsible" persons or units are asked to contribute to the objective in the ways and at the times decided by those with prime responsibility (on the basis of the policies agreed during the deployment phase). These requirements will have already been defined in terms of implementation of the deployment. These persons may be lower or higher in status than the objective leaders. The choice is made on the basis of the skills required and the opportunities to be exploited. As these are "red" objectives, the people concerned cannot refuse to take part since, by definition, they cannot have things to do which are more important than what is necessary to achieve the priority objectives. The only exceptions are obvious *emergencies*. In any case, since they will be considered co-responsible for the results it is in their interest to contribute to them satisfactorily.

94

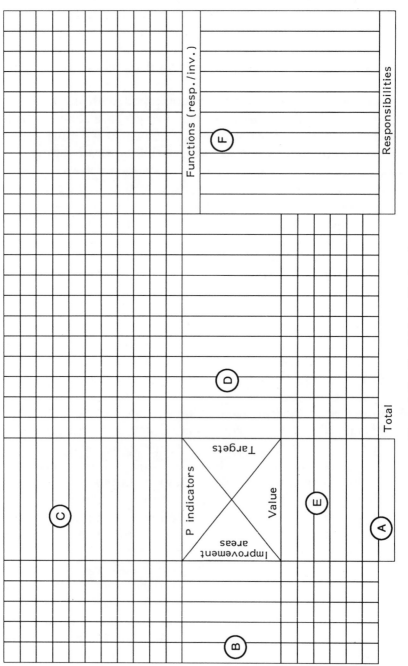

Figure 4.12 The X Matrix (first level).

3 *Availability* (represented by a cross). They are units or persons who can be asked to contribute to an objective in course of achievement, depending on the problems or needs identified by the objective leader. (They are contributions which it has not been possible to identify before the start of operations.)

As mentioned earlier, the X Matrices at the second and third levels are usually more specific and detailed in content. A typical layout is illustrated in Figure 4.13, which gives all the elements usually considered to be necessary for setting up effective operating management. The additional elements compared with the simplified version so far shown are:

- Guidelines/surrounding conditions/constraints
- Organisational arrangements planned for the improvements
- Timetable for developing the improvement actions and for reaching the targets

Guidelines/Surrounding Conditions/Constraints

These are elements useful for the definition of the "hows" agreed for the pursuit of the objectives, to ensure that they are coherent (see the section on strategic planning in Chapter 3). Some examples of guidelines and constraints are given in Figure 4.14 (in the box at the bottom).

Organisational Arrangements for Improvements

These normally fall into the following categories: individual tasks, group projects, SEDAC operations, study groups. These are described below, together with the criteria for their selection according to the type of objective or action to be carried out. In Figure 4.14 it can be seen how the form chosen is set out in the X Matrix.

Timetable

For management to be effective, it is necessary to plan the times for each target or organisational programme. The projects/actions can be planned to run in parallel or in series, depending on the assessment of what is possible or advantageous.

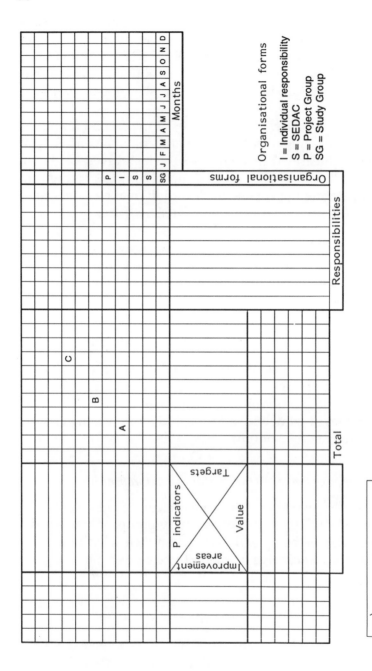

Figure 4.13 The operational X Matrix (basic layout).

Remember that if the actions are to be carried out by the same people, it is more effective to plan, for example, two blocks of five actions in sequence rather than all ten in parallel (effectiveness through focusing).

The contents of the timetable vary according to the organisational arrangement selected:

- If it is an individual task, the complete implementation time should be planned
- If it is a project group, its development phases should be planned (possibly using PDCA)
- If it is a SEDAC, the time necessary to achieve the objective should be planned; in fact, although it has the same nature as a project, SEDAC carries out the PDCA phases in parallel
- If it is a study group, the time assigned to the study and the planning of implementation should be planned

Figure 4.14 gives a planning example. Figures 4.15–4.18 show some examples of X Matrices concerning a variety of objectives and deployment levels. In Figures 4.19 and 4.20 there are two examples which illustrate the complete annual plan. The priority improvement areas at company level, under top management supervision and top-down are given in large letters. The "local" priorities not included in the special management deployment are given in smaller ones. In the firm which has produced these matrices it is considered advisable to use this instrument to "map out" all the activities which it is important to carry out.

Visual Management Using the SEDAC System

As indicated earlier, the X Matrix forms the "bridge" between an objective and its operational management and effective operational management is based on the "visual management" of the entire process launched to achieve the priority objectives. The instruments proposed for this purpose are Master SEDAC and Sub-SEDAC. These are part of the SEDAC system©* developed

---

* SEDAC©: Structure for Enhancing Daily Activities through Creativity.

98

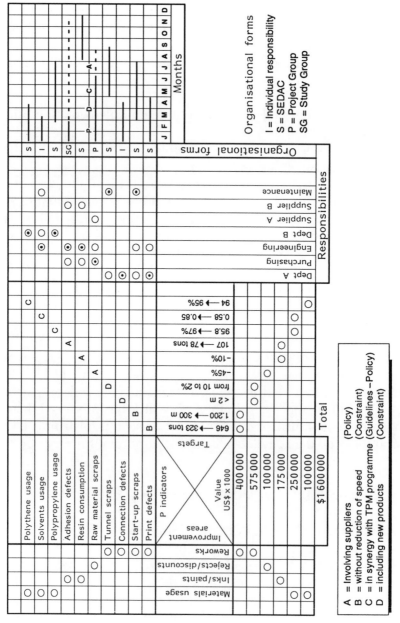

Figure 4.14 The operational X Matrix (third level).

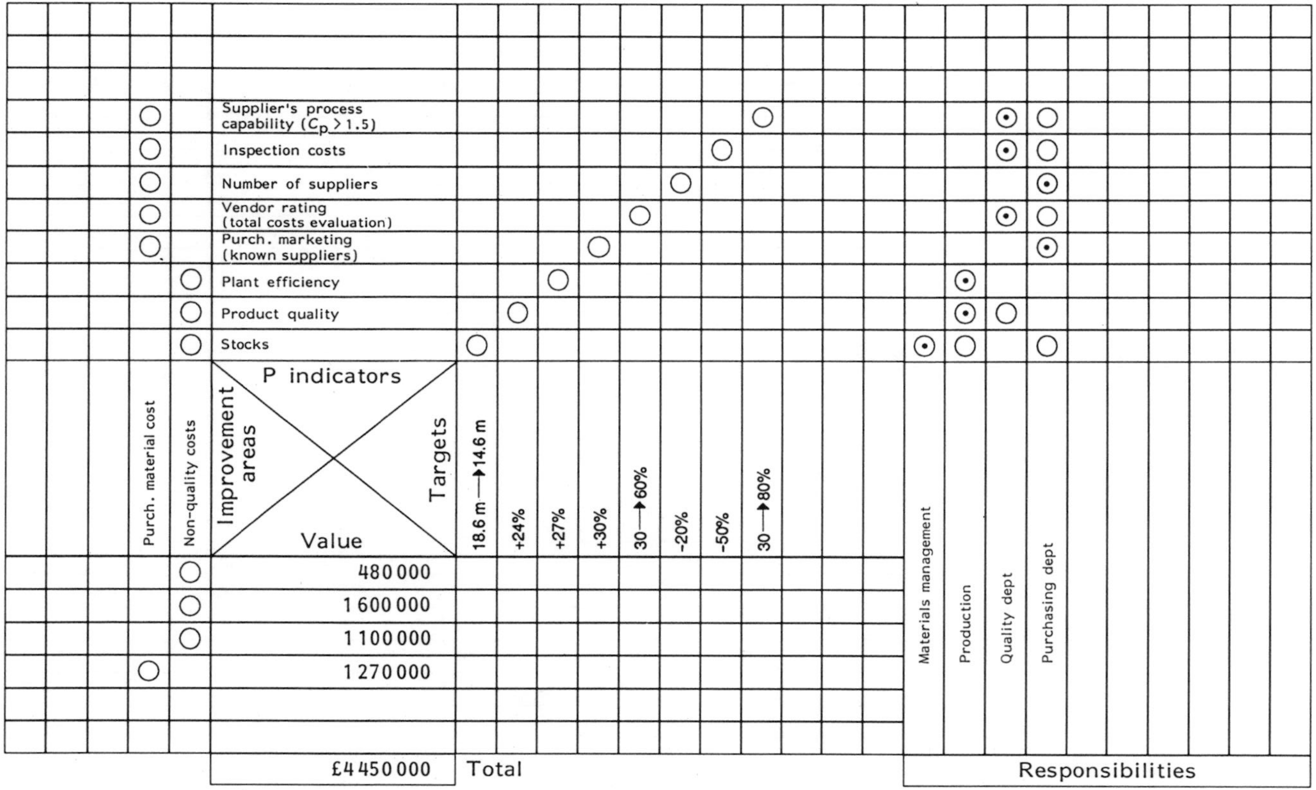

Figure 4.15 A chemical company (first level X matrix). Objective: cost reduction.

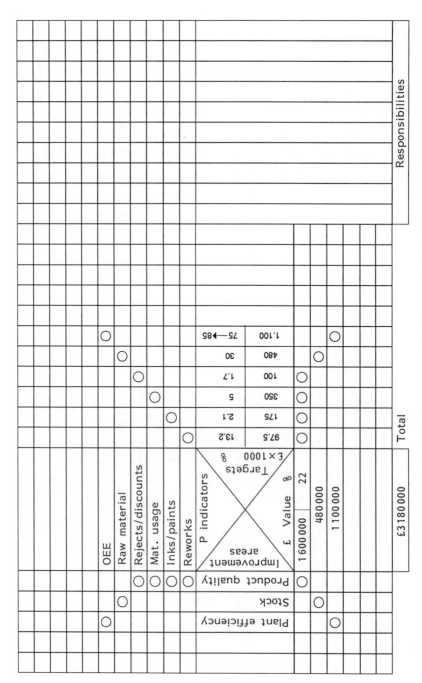

Figure 4.16 A chemical company (second level X matrix). Objective: cost reduction.

101

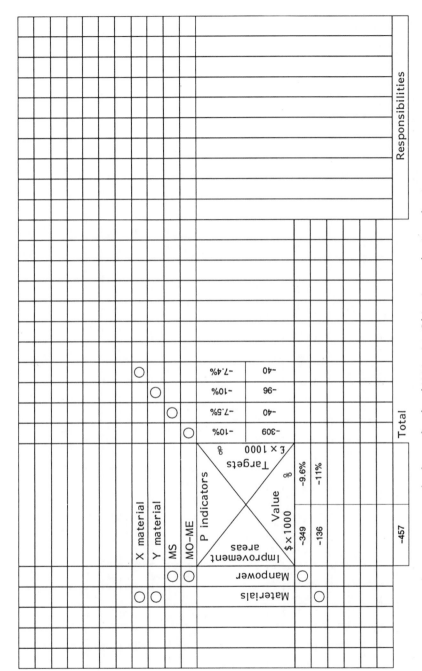

Figure 4.17 An oil refinery (first-level X Matrix). Objective: reduction of maintenance costs.

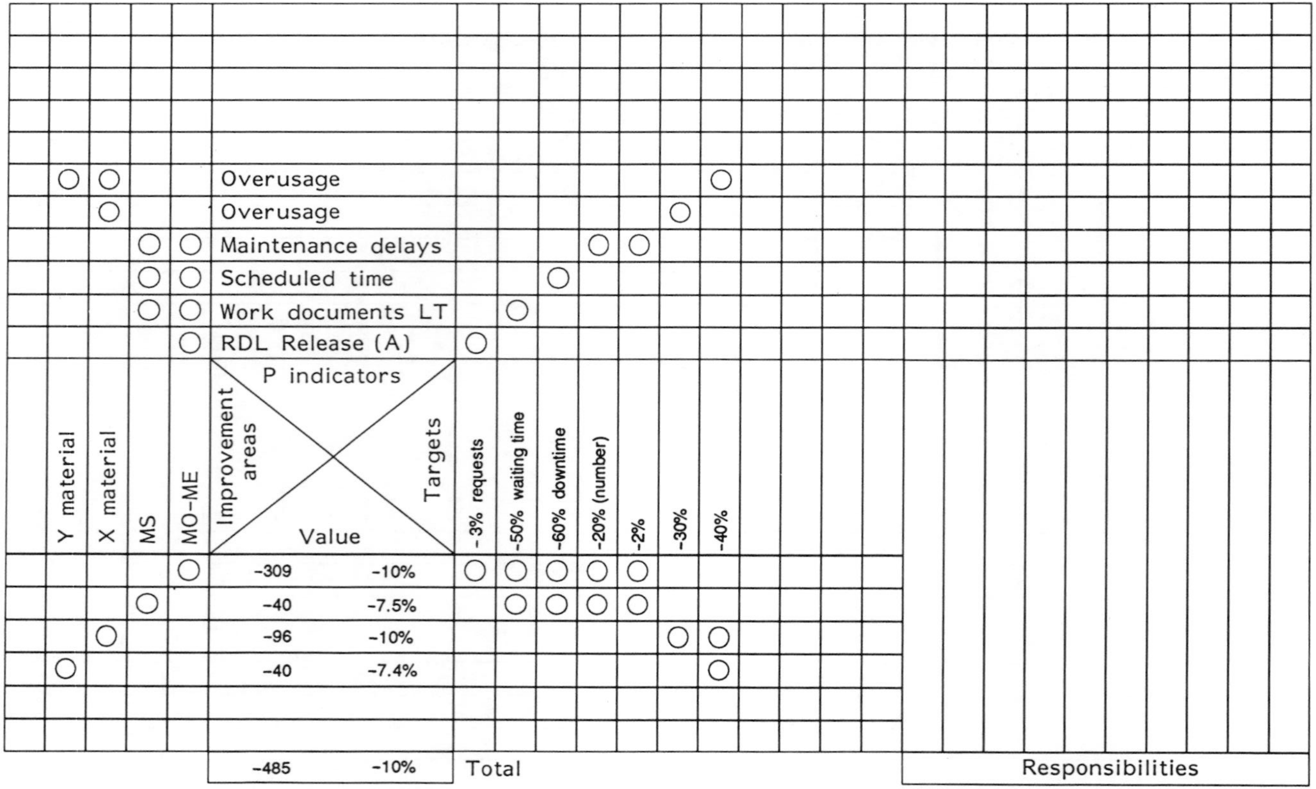

Responsibilities

Total

Targets

- -3% requests
- -50% waiting time
- -60% downtime
- -20% (number)
- -2%
- -30%
- -40%

P indicators

Improvement areas

Value

Improvement areas	Value	Targets
	-10%	-309
	-7.5%	-40
	-10%	-96
	-7.4%	-40
Total	-10%	-485

Overusage
Overusage
Maintenance delays
Scheduled time
Work documents LT
RDL Release (A)

MO-ME
MS
X material
Y material

Figure 4.18 *An oil refinery (second-level X Matrix). Objective: reduction of maintenance costs.*

by Ryuji Fukuda, which also includes Operating SEDAC (see the next chapter) together with Window Analysis and Window Development (discussed in Chapter 5).

The objective of Master and Sub-SEDAC is to *provide all the elements required for the visual management of the performance indicators to be improved and of all the improvement activities which aim to achieve the planned objectives.* These instruments are the practical application of the fundamental principle of breakthrough management, which states that "the main task of managers at all levels is to work every day on the priority objectives of the business, concentrating on the bottlenecks in the process on which their achievement depends". These instruments do in fact overcome the main obstacles to the application of this principle, namely through the possibility to manage by priorities and to identify the bottlenecks and the critical path leading to the priority objectives.

Let us now see how Master and Sub-SEDAC help us to "manage visually by priority". We shall then see how they help us to identify and manage the bottlenecks.

Master SEDAC is the graphical tool for managing the objectives in the first-level X Matrix. It contains the synthesis of the objectives which contribute to the responsibilities of the head of an operating unit or a breakthrough objective. The Master SEDAC is drawn up starting from the indicators and targets of the first-level X Matrix. In the same way, there is a Sub-SEDAC for each second- and third-level X Matrix.

It is, however, only in theory that the number of Master and Sub-SEDAC and the number of X Matrices coincide. The former are in fact only drawn up for the indicators or objectives to which it is sensible to apply visual management. Note the typical pattern of a Master Sub-SEDAC in Figure 4.21 and their link with a scheme of effective management in Figure 4.22 (the meaning of the cards on the SEDAC branches will be explained later).

SEDAC is laid out graphically on a board (say, 1 m × 2 m) visible to all in the office of the manager responsible for the objective, or in the workplace where it must be applied. It is usually a "fishbone" diagram with the indicator of the main objective on the right and those of the sub-objectives (targets) on

Legend:
- ● Main responsible dept
- ◎ Sub-responsible dept
- ○ Related dept

Items (1–14):
1. A MODEL
2. B MODEL
3. C MODEL
4. D PROTOTYPE
5. α LIVE CAPACITY
6. DOWNTIME
7. CEDAC CAMPAIGN
8. PROMOTE D-CEDAC
9. DEVELOP ENG & ADM CEDAC
10. MATERIAL COST
11. FLEXIBLE MFG
12. NEW PRODUCTS START-UP
13. TPM
14. 5S + CAMPAIGN

Objectives:
- New models introduction
- Prod. capacity increase
- ZD campaign
- Cost reduction
- Total productivity
- Safety

Targets:
- Complete within schedule
- Failure cost 50% reduction
- β line rejects
- γ line rejects
- Int. complaints −50%
- Reduction by 30%
- Reduction of overhead by 20%
- From 50% to 80%
- Complete

Departments:
- Production dept
- Engineering dept
- Quality assur. dept
- Administration dept
- Personnel dept
- Display device HQ
- X electronics

Gain: A, B, C, D, E, F — XXX — Total

Figure 4.19 An electronics company. Business plan: president level.

105

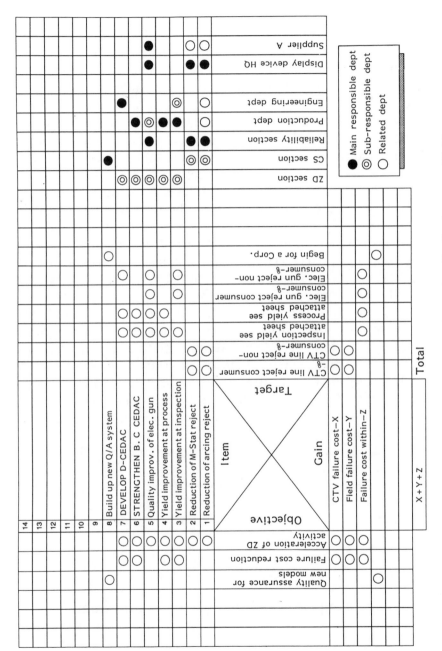

Figure 4.20 An electronics company. Business plan: Quality Assurance Division.

the left. There are, however, other forms of graph which can be used according to the type of objective.

To ensure effective management, the indicator of the overall objective (the "planned" result) should be updated weekly or monthly. The other indicators, of both Master and Sub-SEDACS, should be updated at least weekly if not daily. The company information system is probably incapable of providing the summaries or the breakdowns required to measure the performance to be monitored. Indeed, information systems are usually only designed to report on results whereas the information which we require concerns causes rather than results. In any case, it is difficult to obtain them on a daily basis. If it exists, so much the better! Otherwise, in the majority of cases, the data will be collected "manually".

The fact of having to collect and record data manually every day about our own objectives does have the advantage of ensuring that we stay in close contact with them. In practice they are usually monitored in this way, even in highly computerised firms. It must, however, be remembered that this consists only of a simple sum to be calculated each day for one's "right-hand" SEDAC indicators. The others are updated "bottom-up" by the managers at the next level down (Figure 4.23). The Master SEDAC for our case history and one of its Sub-SEDACs are illustrated in Figure 4.24. In this case the Master SEDAC is the management tool of the factory director, and the Sub-SEDACs belong to the departmental managers.

So far, we have been concerned with organising the visual management of the indicators and the projects to be supervised. We shall see below how these instruments link in with the organisational arrangements created to implement the improvements, and, in particular, how they are used for operating management.

OPERATING

Choosing How to Organise for Improvement

Improvement activities focused on objectives and supervised through the use of Master and Sub-SEDACs are carried out using forms of organisation such as:

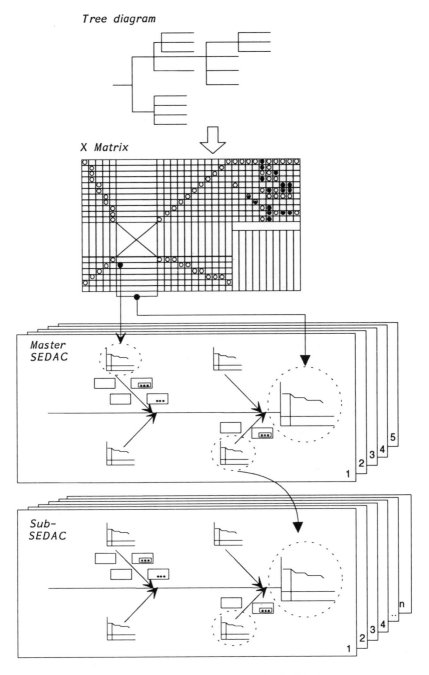

Figure 4.21 *Setting up master and sub-SEDACs.*

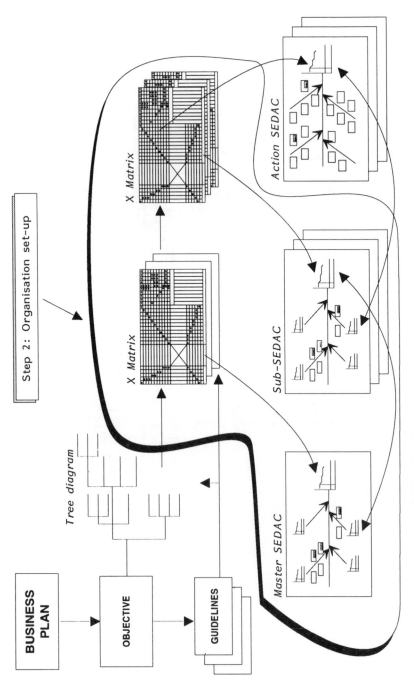

Figure 4.22 *The effective management cycles: organisation set-up.*

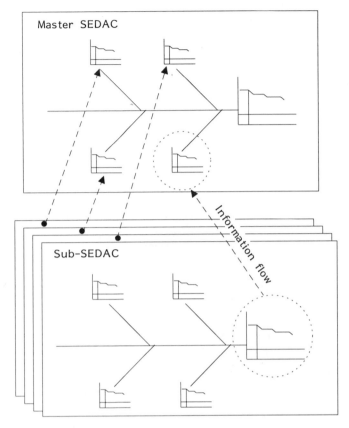

Figure 4.23   *Updating master SEDAC indicators.*

- Individual Tasks
- Project Groups
- Study Groups
- Action SEDAC

These are described below, and we also suggest what should be considered when deciding which of them to use.

Individual Tasks

The responsibility for achieving the target of the project or for carrying out the specific action required is assigned to a single person. Statistically it is the most common form used. It is

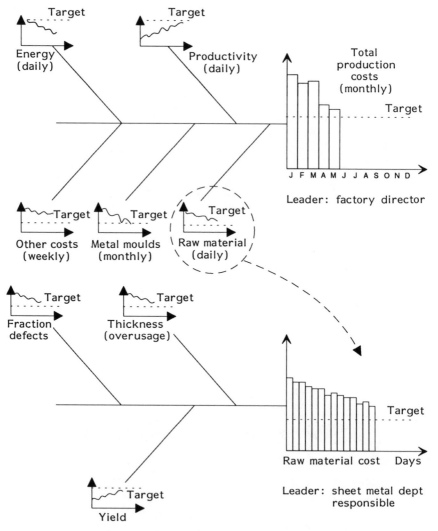

Figure 4.24   *Master and sub-SEDAC in the study case.*

recommended when the actions or projects have a high specialist/technical content, or in the case of relatively simple actions or objectives.

Project Groups

These are groups of three to seven persons, usually middle managers from different functions, selected to tackle an improvement project. They use the *problem-finding* and *problem-solving* methodologies of the PDCA process (see Merli, Euro-challenge IFS 1993). They meet regularly (usually every one or two weeks), coordinated by a leader who either has been appointed or has been elected by the group. The group is dissolved at the end of the project (which should not last more than four to six months, under penalty of losing its effectiveness). Project Groups should only be used for innovative or complex projects since they are usually cumbersome and time consuming.

Study Groups

These are made up of more senior managers or of persons of outstanding competence, and are almost always multifunctional. They are used when it is not clear how an objective should be tackled and an "investigation" is necessary to arrive at a decision. It is a first-phase organisation which should lead to one of the three other types of organisation described, depending on the approach selected. This phase should not last more than a month.

Action SEDAC

This form of organisation is probably the most modern and effective (it is used by almost all the firms quoted in the first part of the book as examples of success). This does not mean that it can be used universally. It is employed when it is the performance of existing activities which must be improved, through the upgrading of the operating methods already in use in the firm. It is not suitable for innovative projects (for which Project Groups are recommended). It is the type of organisation which should be the most common after Individual Tasks, since it concerns the most common type of improvement. Many of the projects which firms assign today to Project Groups or Improvement Groups would be better handled by this type of organisation.

Experience demonstrates that by using this approach the effectiveness of improvement activities could be increased tenfold. It is certainly true that the time taken to develop a project using Action SEDAC is about a third of that taken by a group. In addition a SEDAC project takes two or three months compared with the three to six months which are the statistical range for a Project Group.

For a more analytical description of the criteria to be applied when choosing a type of organisation, see the above section on "Mobilisation capacity".

Since it is both new and important, Action SEDAC is the only type of organisation which needs to be described in detail in this book.

Managing Improvement using SEDAC

Action SEDAC is the final element required to complete the breakthrough management process proposed in this book. As can be seen in Figure 4.25, it provides the tool for transforming the two previous phases of "planning" and "organising management" into operating reality. It is directly inserted into the cascade down from the Master SEDAC and Sub-SEDACs which are its origin, as illustrated in Figure 4.26. Action SEDAC belongs to the family of SEDAC System instruments developed by Ryuji Fukuda. SEDAC,* as mentioned earlier, is an acronym derived from Structure for Enhancing Daily Activities through Creativity.

The operating system is based on the generous use of Post-it type "cards". The operating tools of the system (Action SEDAC) consists of various types of diagram called "SEDAC Diagrams". These are boards on view in the offices or departments where there is the problem to be eliminated or the performance to be improved.

In breakthrough management the point of departure for a SEDAC diagram is the lowest-level indicator identified in the deployment process, that is, an indicator and target from a branch of a Sub-SEDAC. In our study case it could, for example, be attached to the objective "yield improvement". The link with the Sub-SEDAC and the Master SEDAC which are its source is illustrated in Figure 4.27.

---

* The copyright of the SEDAC System for Europe and South America is the property of Galgano & Associates.

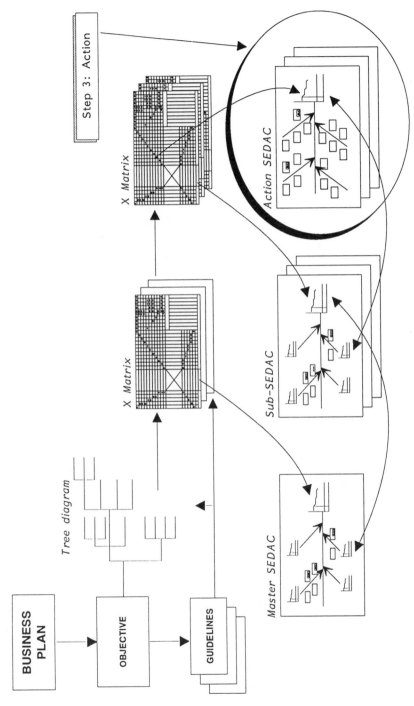

Figure 4.25 The effective management cycle: action.

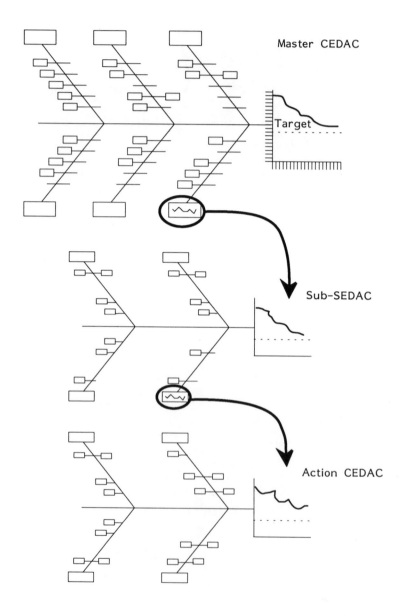

Figure 4.26   *SEDACs in cascade.*

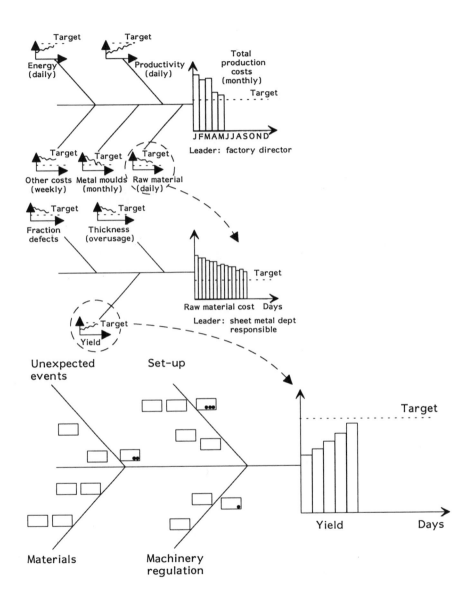

Figure 4.27 *SEDACs in cascade in the study case.*

There are various forms of SEDAC diagrams designed for different types of objectives, such as:

• CEDAC®* (Cause-and-Effect Diagram with Addition of Cards—Figure 4.28). the most widely used diagram, designed to highlight cause-and-effect relationships. i.e. the problems and obstacles in the way of the improvement sought
• PERTAC (a combination of SEDAC and a PERT diagram— Figure 4.29). Very useful for "make to order" processes (engineering or production) where it is necessary to concentrate on critical paths
• FLOWAC (a combination of SEDAC and a flow diagram— Figure 4.30). recommended where the improvement concerns a process or a procedure
• FMEI (Failure Mode Effect Improvement—Figure 4.31). Combines FMEA and SEDAC to tackle objectives of product or process reliability improvement

Of all the SEDAC diagrams the most widely employed is certainly CEDAC. We will now use it to illustrate how a SEDAC diagram physically "works".

The CEDAC® Diagram†

The CEDAC® diagram is a methodology which enables the improvement process to be brought to the workstation and to be part of the everyday life of managers, foremen and the workforce. It also makes it possible to involve a large number of people in improvement activities with only a minimum of meetings.

The CEDAC diagram is a very flexible instrument which can be used to manage a variety of situations:

• Organisation and definition of the individual improvement activities

---

* The copyright of the CEDAC diagram for Europe is the property of Galgano & Associates and for Britain, France and USA of Productivity Inc.
† Written by Carlalberto Da Pozzo, Galgano & Associates.

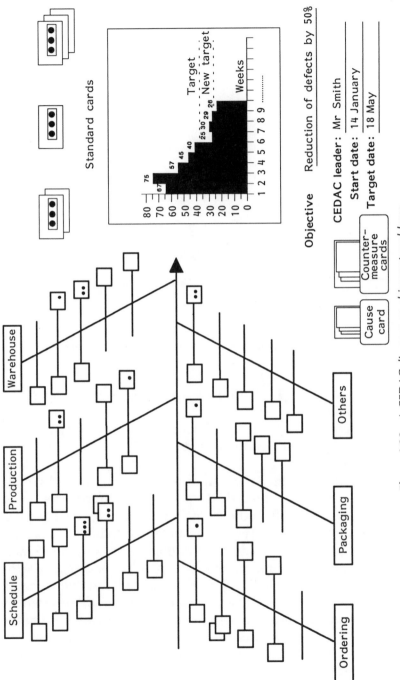

Figure 4.28 *A CEDAC diagram on shipment problems.*

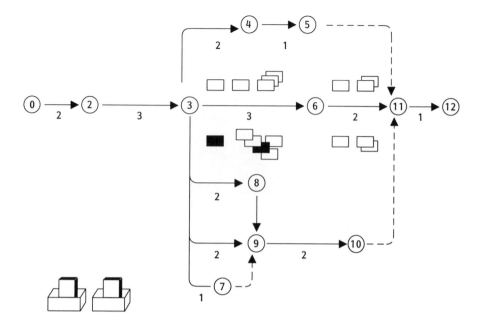

Figure 4.29   *PERTAC (Programme Evaluation and Review Technique + SEDAC).*

- Supervision and continuous improvement of operating performances
- Improvement projects (when not purely innovative)
- Standardisation of improvement

Physically the CEDAC diagram is a board located where the problem has to be solved or the activity improved. The board must be visible to all, and everyone must have access to it. It is divided into two parts (Figure 4.32): the "effects" side and the "causes" (or "levers") side. On the effects side we put the most suitable indicators for monitoring the problem or objective ("the object of improvement"). These are usually in the form of graphs updated daily. This allows all interested parties to have the performance improvement trend constantly in view. On the causes/levers side we put the elements which prevent the improvement or create the problem and also ideas on how to solve it. Anyone can indicate on cards what are the *obstacles* found which prevent the improvement from taking place and/or what

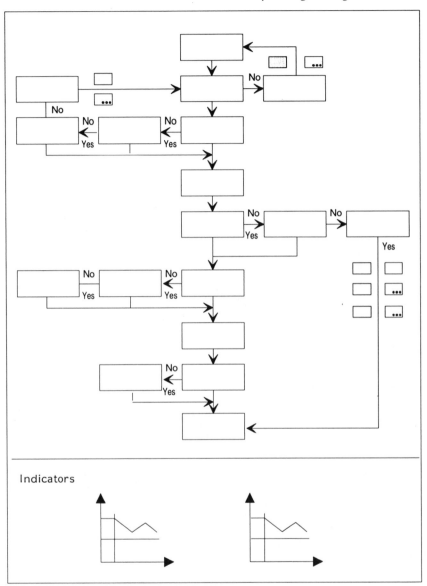

Figure 4.30   *Flow diagram + SEDAC (FLOWAC).*

remedies could be applied to overcome them. These notes are made on different coloured cards (indicating cause or remedy).

The leader responsible for the project or objective will test the ideas which he or she finds the most interesting. The results of

120

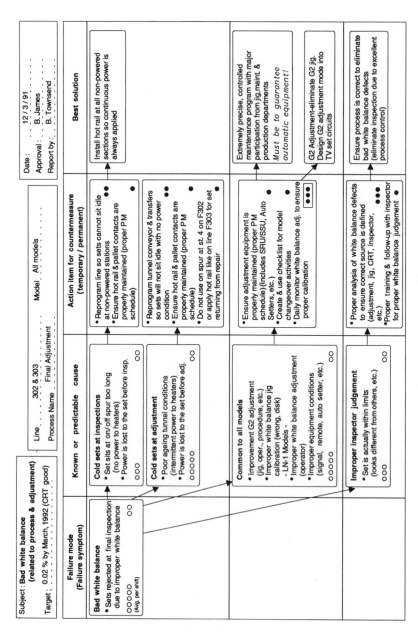

Subject : **Bad white balance**
(related to process & adjustment)
Target : 0.02 % by March, 1992 (CRT good)

Line . . . . . . 302 & 303 . . . . . . Model . All models . . . . .
Process Name . . Final Adjustment . . .

Date : . . . . 12 / 3 / 91 . . . .
Approval : . . . . B. James . . . .
Report by : . . B. Townsend . . . . . .

Failure mode (Failure symptom)	Known or predictable cause	Action item for countermeasure (temporary / permanent)	Best solution
Bad white balance • Sets rejected at final inspection due to improper white balance OOOOO OO (Avg. per shift)	**Cold sets at inspections** • Set sits at on/off spur too long (no power to heaters) • Power is lost to the set before insp. OO OO	• Reprogram line so sets cannot sit idle at non-powered stations ● ● • Ensure hot rail & pallet contacts are properly maintained (proper PM schedule) ●	Install hot rail at all non-powered sections so continuous power is always applied
	Cold sets at adjustment • Poor ageing tunnel conditions (intermittent power to heaters) • Power is lost to the set before adj. OOOOO OO	• Reprogram tunnel conveyor & transfers so sets will not sit idle with no power condition ● ● • Ensure hot rail & pallet contacts are properly maintained (proper PM schedule) ● • Do not use on spur at st. 4 on F302 or apply hot rail like on line F303 for set returning from repair	
	Common to all models • Improvement G2 adjustment (jig, oper., procedure, etc.) • Improper white balance jig calibration (wrong, disk) - LN-1 Models - • Improper white balance adjustment (operator) • Improper equipment conditions (signal, remote, auto setter, etc.) OOOOO OO	• Ensure adjustment equipment is properly maintained (proper PM schedule) (includes SRU/SSU, Auto Setters, etc.) ● • Create & use checklist for model changeover activities ● • Daily monitor white balance adj. to ensure proper calibration ● ● ●	Extremely precise, controlled maintenance program with major participation from jig, maint & production departments *Must be to guarantee automatic equipment!* G2 Adjustment-eliminate G2 jig. Design G2 adjustment mode into TV set circuits
	Improper inspector judgement • Set is actually within limits (looks different from others, etc.) OOO OO	• Proper analysis of white balance defects to ensure correct source is defined (adjustment, jig, CRT, inspector, etc.) ● ● ● • Proper training & follow-up with inspector for proper white balance judgement ●	Ensure process is correct to eliminate bad white balance defects (eliminate inspection due to excellent process control)

Figure 4.31 FMEI table.

these experiments will be evaluated using the indicators which monitor the problem. If the ideas are successful, the improvement is obvious to all. In other words, the CEDAC diagram makes it possible to:

- Constantly call the attention of everyone to an important problem or target that the firm "wishes" to tackle (identified through breakthrough management deployment)
- Collect a large amount of information about the real causes of a problem or obstacles to an improvement
- Stimulate the generation, collection and consideration of the ideas of a number of people without having to call meetings
- Inform everyone in real time about the improvements under way and about the introduction of new standards

The setting up and administration of the CEDAC diagram is carried out in seven basic phases, some concerning the effects side and others the causes/levers side (Figure 4.32). These are:

1 Identify the parameters to be used for measuring the results of the improvement actions and their impact on the objective (the indicators)
2 Define the frequency of data collection for the indicators
3 Define the objectives (targets) for the indicators
4 Collect the cards concerning the obstacles/problems (the reasons which prevent the target from being reached)
5 Collect the cards with the improvement ideas (how to overcome the problems/obstacles)
6 Select and test the improvement ideas (try out what appear to be the most valid ideas)
7 Define and apply the new standards (to make the improvements irreversible).

The CEDAC board is administered by a "CEDAC leader" (who is responsible for that specific CEDAC), the person to whom the company board (or the "boss") has assigned the problem or improvement to be tackled. He or she plays a decisive role in the correct use of the diagram and in the effective application of the improvement process.

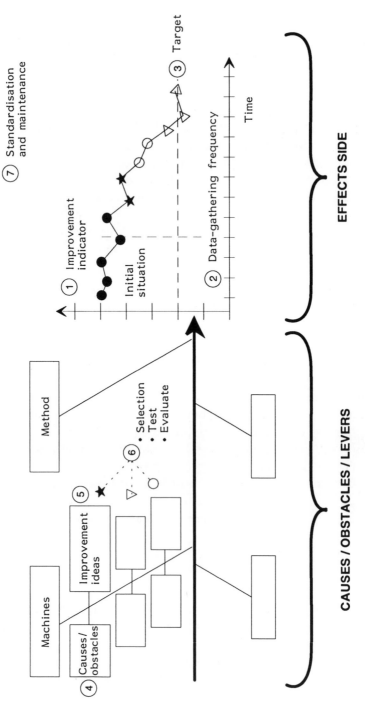

Figure 4.32 Setting up a CEDAC diagram.

The CEDAC leader is responsible for organising and managing the diagram and coordinating all related activities. He or she should have a detailed knowledge of the problem/improvement area, and be a leader both in status and in personal qualities. The main tasks are to:

- Promote the activity
- Design and organise the board
- Analyse the obstacle cards
- Evaluate the improvement idea cards (see Figure 4.33)
- Test the improvement ideas considered suitable (eventually with other units)
- Standardise the effective ideas

It is important to emphasise that the CEDAC leader does not have to do all this, but must be able to ensure that each phase is carried out correctly, using whoever he or she thinks most suitable.

The advantage of the CEDAC diagram can be seen from the following points of view:

1 *The large number of people involved* The diagram makes everyone aware of an important problem or objective, attracts their attention and involvement (quite apart from taking an active part by putting cards on the board). It stimulates and brings together everyone's ideas on the problem and its solution, and the dynamics of the process do a great deal to integrate the various levels and functions (including staff and line). The diagram is visible to all and everyone has access to the definition of standards. It stimulates and generates a large volume of inputs into the diagnosis and the improvement activity.

2 *The operating method* Since it takes cause-and-effect relationships as its focal point the method continuously consolidates this approach in practice. It provides everyone with immediate feedback on the results obtained and creates a concrete, immediate sense of achievement. Everyone involved knows the process which has developed the standards, and how they affect the parameters of the process. Finally, it helps to diffuse the new standards.

3   *The development of the improvement culture*   Since it develops the concept of continuous improvement on a daily basis, the diagram helps to integrate improvement and day-to-day tasks, so that improvement becomes a normal, routine activity.

The CEDAC diagram is the *basic tool* for implementing the breakthrough management process. In Figures 4.34, 4.35 and 4.36 we give some practical examples of CEDAC.

MONITORING AND MANAGING

Approach

Of the four phases of breakthrough management (planning/programming, organising management, operating, monitoring and managing), it is the last phase, monitoring and management, which converts all the potential created in the other phases into "breakthrough management". This is the dynamic stage which brings to life all the instruments previously set up. It transforms the scheme in Figure 4.37 into an operating management system.

No new tools or methodologies are introduced at this stage. It is a question of organising what has been created so far so that it focuses on the projected breakthrough. The management objective is therefore to build an effective system for monitoring and managing operating activities which makes it possible to:

- Manage priorities in "real time" (day by day)
- Monitor the priority objective indicators "visually"
- Identify current bottlenecks which are preventing objectives from being achieved
- Manage the bottlenecks effectively

Let us see how this objective can be achieved.

Monitoring

As we have said earlier, "real-time" information is a condition *sine qua non* of breakthrough management. The information flow

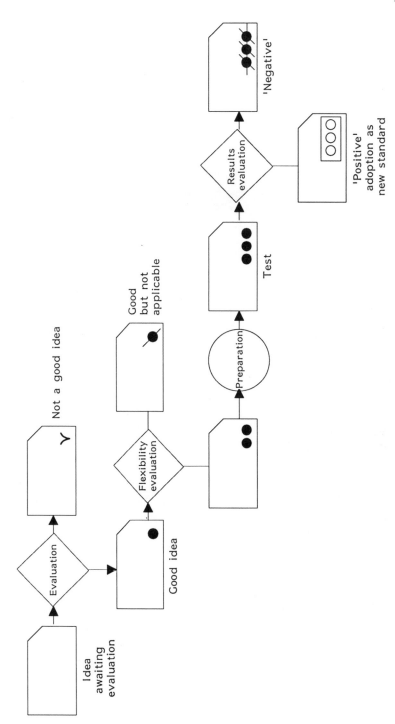

Figure 4.33 Cards evaluation scheme.

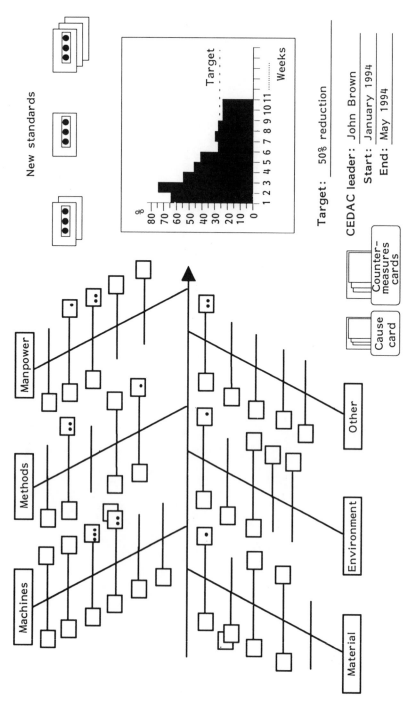

Figure 4.34 CEDAC project: reduction of surface scratches.

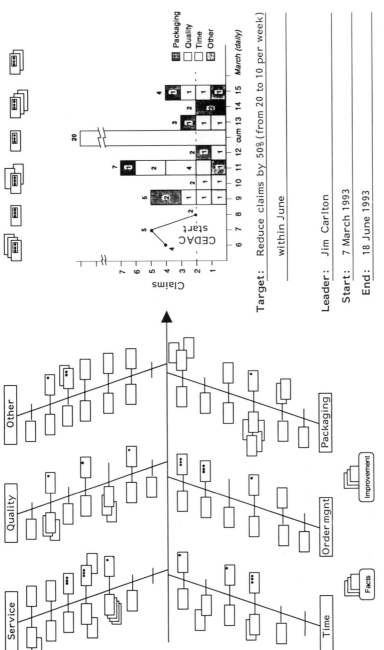

Figure 4.35 *CEDAC diagram: claims reduction.*

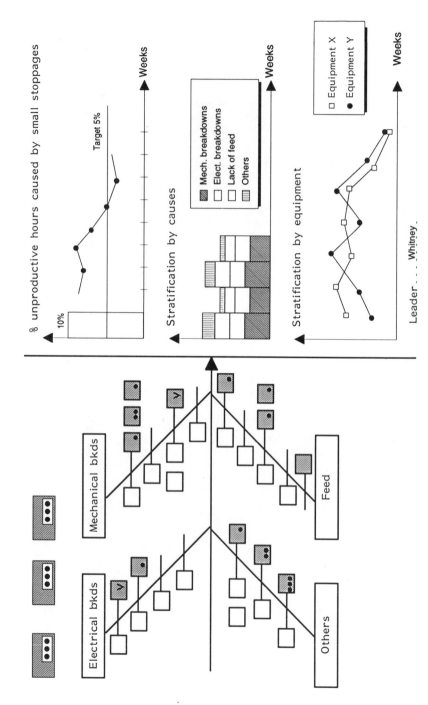

Figure 4.36 *CEDAC project: increase in yield (automatic machines).*

for this purpose is based on the cascade framework of SEDAC and transports the management information to the right places in the following way.

Updating of Management Information (Figure 4.38)

This is done using an implosive type of information flow with consolidations at each level upwards through the organisation, following the opposite of the deployment flow of the indicators (i.e. from the particular to the general). This means that daily or weekly each SEDAC leader has to update the indicator linked to his or her objective simultaneously on two graphs: the right-hand side of the leader's SEDAC and that of the branch of the Sub-SEDAC from which it originated.

The same will happen between the Sub-SEDAC and the Master SEDAC. Similar information must be provided by the other types of improvement organisation such as Project Groups and Individual Tasks. The information can be transmitted upward in various ways:

- Computer network (if available)
- Photocopy
- Fax
- Telephone
- Direct recording on the diagram of the level above

The type of flow is illustrated on the right-hand side of Figure 4.38.

This updating process allows the Master and Sub-SEDAC leaders to check day by day which performance is the most critical and, by using the cascade, what are the causes. By following the *indicators' critical path* they are able to identify which is the area currently most critical to the priority objective, and concentrate on precisely those bottlenecks which must be the priorities of the moment.

Information on Problems/ideas/new standards

At the same time as they transmit performance data for the indicators, the SEDAC and Sub-SEDAC leaders are also asked to

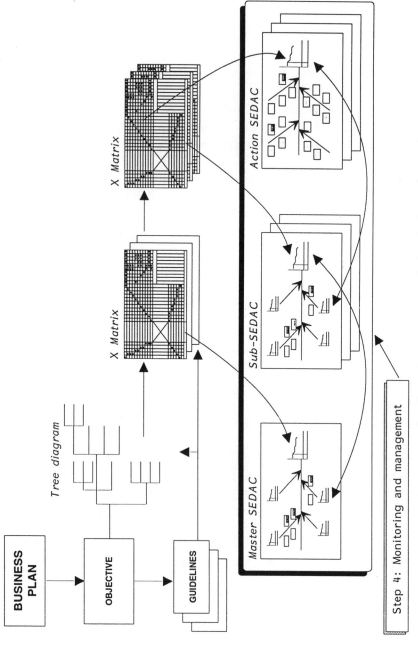

Figure 4.37 *The effective management cycle: monitoring and managing.*

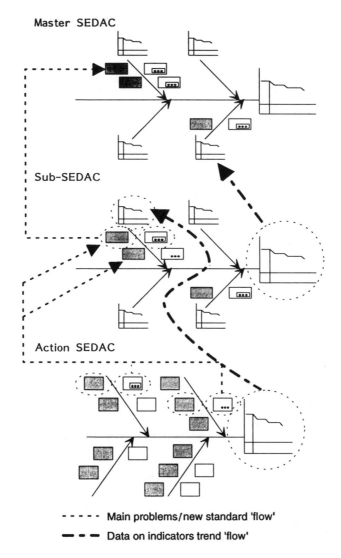

Figure 4.38 *Information flow—updating the SEDAC indicators.*

send information upwards regarding *major obstacles*, the *main ideas*, and new standards introduced. This allows objectives leaders at the next level up to have "real-time" information on the main problems arising, what is being done about them, and what new standards have been introduced, all without waiting for reports (always late) or calling meetings (always costly and difficult to organise). The bottom-up flow of this type of information is illustrated on the left-hand side of Figure 4.38.

Information on Improvement Activities

This can be partly extrapolated from the previous flow. If major problems have actually been reported it is highly likely that some remedies can be found—all the better if important ideas/remedies or even new standards have already been identified. Another type of information which we need is the number of obstacle cards and idea cards collected. This is transmitted at the same time as the previous information, and gives an idea as to whether and to what extent the improvement activity is under way. The information is very important for breakthrough management. We have already seen how much this depends on the "upstream management" of what can generate the desired improvement to the outputs.

Therefore, if it is true that by selecting indicators measuring causes and not results, management can concentrate on the variables which determine the desired result, it will be even more effective if it can concentrate on the activities which aim to make those improvements. It is hopeless to expect the performance of the "cause" variables to improve if there is no improvement activity aimed at doing so.

It is evident that this management approach allows results to be managed "two steps upstream" (that is, by managing the activities which can improve the performance of the causes which determine the performance that we want to improve). It therefore ensures *greater effectiveness* (because it is acting on the improvement levers of the causes) and *quicker results* (because it acts earlier). We could add that it manages yet another step upstream, by identifying the problems or obstacles which must be removed if improvement is to take place.

How can we improve performance if we do not know what to tackle? It is not by accident that the Japanese call the problems "treasures". If we did not first dig up the problems, we should not be able to launch any improvement activity, since we should not know what to aim at.

Knowing this we can perhaps understand the reasons for the great success of Japanese industry, which as an institution is focused on the improvement of the process variables that produce business results, through the meticulous removal of the slightest problem. It should also enable us to understand better the real *difference between management and management control*: the former is focused on causes, the latter on results.

Finally it should be remembered that for the complete improvement process to be managed visually, the bottom-up information cards should also carry information on the improvement activities taking place outside SEDAC (through Project Groups, Individual Tasks, etc.)

Operating Management

"Operating management" is the point in the breakthrough management process which brings into use all the potential created in the preceding phases, including monitoring. It should let us *identify the bottlenecks of the moment which are getting in the way of the priority objectives, and take the right measures to remove them.* Using the proposed system we can pursue the first of these objectives through a mixture of several operating methods:

- Management by "critical indicators"
- Management by "critical flows"
- "Patrol"

Management by Critical Indicators

The process is illustrated by the following possible situation. The Master SEDAC leader (the factory director in our example) will make a monthly check of total production costs on the right-hand indicator of his Master SEDAC, to check the coherence between the improvement made and therefore the results expected, and the actual results achieved. Discrepancies would probably call into question the validity of the deployment itself, and could lead to a decision that it should be revised. But his main task is what he does weekly or daily, which is to check the progress of the sub-indicators entered on his Master SEDAC. It is in this way that he can be aware of the most critical indicator of the moment in relation to planned results. He will then detach the graph (usually on an A4 sheet) which indicates the critical performance and go down to see its leader (of the Sub-SEDAC concerned) so that they can assess the reasons for the sub-standard improvement. Together they will try to find the most critical sub-indicator in the Sub-SEDAC (probably already "assessed" by its leader) and so on, until in an Action SEDAC they identify the main cause of the problem or sub-performance. We shall see later what the leaders should do once they have arrived at the problem.

Management by Critical Flow

The Master SEDAC leader must also make a daily examination of the information coming in from the problems/ideas/new standards cards (the main ones and the quantitative data). If the operating indicators discussed above do not show any relative problems (i.e. none of them is worse than the others), the bottleneck of the moment must be sought using this type of information. The following situations may be found:

- *An insufficient flow of cards (or even none)*   It is clear that in this case it would be difficult for performance to improve. If there has been an improvement, it is probably because of the greater attention focused on it as being performance "under observation". But this is a particularly "delicate" situation. If the improvement is not due to any specific change, it will probably disappear as soon as it is no longer under a spotlight. Therefore something must be done, but what is the bottleneck? It is probably the leaders at operating level who do not know how to get an improvement process going. It is on them and on their capacity to create participation that the Master SEDAC leader must concentrate.
- *Only "obstacles" cards*   In this case the Master SEDAC leader must find ways of stimulating the diagnostic skills, the creativity or the improvement organisation capabilities of the line management concerned (later we shall see how this can be done).
- *Only "obstacles" and "ideas" cards, but no new standards*   In this case the leaders are probably failing to move the organisation in order to implement the ideas, or else the ideas are very weak (in which case, back to the previous case).

- *Cards with obstacles or ideas to which the experience or know how of the senior leaders can make a contribution* In this case the "boss" joins in and takes part in the improvement activities directly on the spot, as a consultant. These are situations which the leaders consider they must "freeze" since they are potentially damaging, usually for reasons well known to them.

"Patrol"

This is an activity with a flow opposite to those above, being carried out bottom-up instead of top-down. It is performed weekly or monthly by every Master or Sub-SEDAC leader (including the top manager of the operating unit) to help the organisation in its improvement activities from the bottom (to "improve its improvement capabilities"). This sort of operation, besides showing *commitment* to the activity and the objective, aims to bring concrete help to the weak links in the organisation. These weak links are mainly identified by assessing the activities of each Action SEDAC during systematic "patrols" of the operating sections (production and offices). The main activity is to coach the middle managers involved in the improvement activities. But is not unusual to come across genuinely important operating problems or improvement opportunities.

The methods for managing the bottleneck discovered by this means must be found through analysis of the nature of the problem. In the firms which have gone furthest in the use of the SEDAC System, this is systematically carried out through "Window Analysis". At Sony, for example, it is considered to be the basic mechanism for breakthrough management. This instrument is described in Chapter 5.

There are, of course, simpler ways of doing this based on the professional capacities of the managers involved, which can in the first instance replace a "scientific" approach. The purpose of the diagnosis is to identify the nature of the problem or obstacle which is creating the *bottleneck*. In fact its removal or remedy depends a great deal on this diagnosis. As an example:

- If the cause of the problem is not known we must immediately set up a study group to tackle it (or, even better, a *task force* in the case of a priority objective)

- If it is already known in the firm *how* to avoid the problem but not in the area in question, the method must be properly explained to its staff
- If, on the other hand, everyone knows in theory how to avoid the problem, but in practice they fail to do so, adequate training of the staff is required
- If it is an improvement which is not being tackled properly in terms of method, it is probably necessary to set up a specific Action SEDAC or other form of organisation

Let us simplify the description of this important moment for management, that is, "how to tackle priority bottlenecks", by giving a few practical recipes which can be used if the complete operating system is based on SEDAC diagrams. Let us examine them according to the causes which managers may find themselves faced with when they identify the bottleneck:

1   *A large number of problems/obstacles have been reported on the bottleneck* (for example, a large number of cards on the left-hand side of the CEDAC branch), but without any ideas on how to improve the situation. In this case the manager should be able to establish:
    - *Whether the problem/obstacle is really unknown*   Then the manager should straight away set up a study task force, involving everyone necessary, at whatever level. This is possible because of the level in the structure of the Master SEDAC leader, and is justified by the importance of the problem (the bottleneck of a business priority).
    - *Whether there are no ideas because of the weakness of the Action SEDAC leader*   In this case the Master SEDAC leader must try to understand whether it is through a lack of commitment, of motivation or of capacity, and take action in consequence. In the last case (incapacity) the Master SEDAC should focus on how to help the leader, and not show up his or her inadequacies (that can come later . . . the immediate priority is how best to tackle the problem!).
2   *On the bottleneck both obstacles and ideas considered valid are recorded but these have not been tested, or the remedies demonstrated to be valid have not been engineered or applied because of the slowness of one or other of the units involved* (for example,

Purchasing, Accounts, Organisation, Tooling, etc.).* In this case the authority and status of the Master SEDAC leader should be used to start up what has not yet been launched, bypassing normal procedures if necessary ("the priority end justifies the exceptional means").

3 *On the bottleneck* (the entire Action SEDAC or one if its branches) *there are no problems/obstacles or idea cards.* In this case the problem is similar to the first one, but much more serious. The diagnosis is very simple: the Action SEDAC leader is failing to deal with the problem. Very probably what he is basically lacking is the capacity to involve his staff in the improvement process, although his own diagnostic capacity could also be a problem (otherwise he would at least have found something!). A major or drastic remedy is required: either he switches the SEDAC leader, or he dedicates all the time it may take to help him (for example, one or two hours a day for at least a week). It is worth it, as we are talking about a priority problem!

It can be seen that what is proposed makes minimum use of meetings or working groups (but when it does, the result is very effective) or of paperwork, accounting or EDP systems. Instead it is based on management:

- In real time
- Focused on the causes/levers of the problems/improvements (and not on the results)
- Attacking the bottlenecks of the objectives
- Free as far as possible from bureaucratic procedures and the constraints of the management hierarchy
- Capable of using the skills required at the right moment

This system, even in its most "naive" form as presented here, should make it easier to meet what we stated to be the requirement of effective operating management, that is:

---

* In the SEDAC diagrams these situations are identified by one, two or three circles on the remedies/ideas cards. Analysis is therefore very easy.

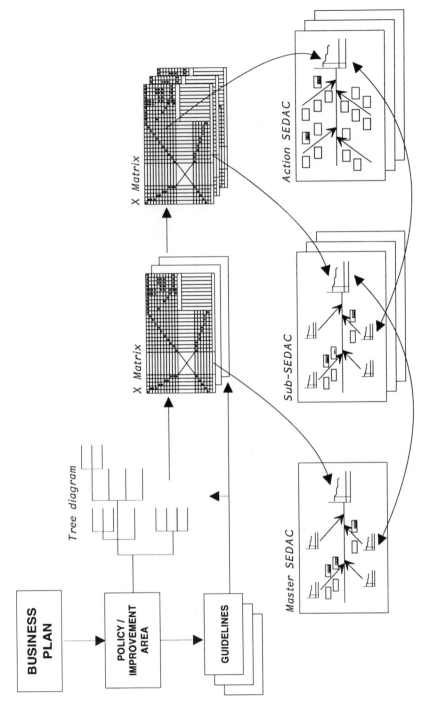

Figure 4.39 *The effective management cycle.*

- *To be capable of managing priorities "in real time"* (through the continuous supervision of the operating indicators monitoring the variables of the business processes concerned)
- *To be capable of "visual supervision" of the indicators of the priority objectives* (which is possible thanks to the SEDAC cascade system)
- *To be capable of finding the current bottlenecks blocking the priority objectives* (through the methodologies provided for this purpose by the SEDAC system)
- *To be capable of dealing effectively with the bottlenecks* (thanks to the Window Analysis methodology or its substitutes)

This completes our description of the last phase of the breakthrough management process, which we have called "monitoring and managing". It should now be more clear what are the methods which translate the proposed breakthrough management framework into practice, and which we reproduce again in conclusion (Figure 4.39).

SUMMARY

The breakthrough objectives plan formulated during the preparation of the annual plan (Chapter 3) is the object of a special management process which allows the managers to:

1   Identify priority operating objectives
2   Assign the right responsibilities
3   Identify the most appropriate operating indicators and targets
4   Manage priorities "in real time" (day by day)
5   Supervise "visually" the indicators of the priority objectives
6   Find the current bottlenecks blocking the priority objectives
7   Deal effectively with these bottlenecks

This translates into practice the basic principle of breakthrough management, which is that: "the main task of a boss at each level is to work every day on the priority business objectives, and to concentrate on removing the bottlenecks to the process on which their achievement depends". We have described the physical application of the breakthrough management process which consists of four operating phases:

1. Planning and programming objectives
2. Organising management
3. Operating
4. Monitoring and managing

The basic instruments used in this process are the X Matrix and the SEDAC system. We have also described some typical examples of how to manage the process.

5
Approaches and Supporting Instruments

INTRODUCTION

In this chapter we present approaches and instruments which are useful when we apply the breakthrough management process. We describe three of these, respecting the criteria often quoted in this book: concentrate on a few things, the most important, the most useful (and in this case, the least well known). We have selected:

- Theory of Constraints
- Affinity Diagram
- Window Analysis/Development

for the following reasons:

1   The Theory of Constraints is a global, "sophisticated" approach (not simple, but highly effective), used for carrying out major diagnoses. It is an approach to be used when we have to identify what should be tackled if we want to achieve a genuine breakthrough in the performance of the business. It is particularly useful when the problem is to decide which type of improvement gives the greatest leverage, rather than what is the size of the improvement.

2   The Affinity Diagram is an alternative way of starting up the breakthrough management process when it is not possible to carry out an accurate deployment starting from business priorities, or when priority is given to existing problems.

3   Window Analysis/Development is a methodology which is complementary to the SEDAC System instruments already described. It is perhaps the only scientific instrument available today for making a good on-site analysis of the nature of the problems encountered, and a rapid, logical decision on how they should be tackled.

THE THEORY OF CONSTRAINTS*

Introduction

If we want to make a real impact on the results of our business, we must be able to answer two basic questions:

1   *What should we change?* (i.e. identify the factors and the objectives which have the greatest impact on the results of the business)

2   *How should we make the changes?* (i.e. identify the levers and the actions necessary to convert objectives into results).

An effective way of answering these questions is provided by the *Theory of Constraints,* a highly innovative approach developed by Eliyahu M. Goldratt (author of *The Goal,* a book which has already sold over a million copies). The theory is based on the observation that the results of any organisation depend on the *weakest link* in the chain of its activities. But what is often lacking is precisely this awareness of the factors or business areas which are the weakest links. The fundamental key to the success of the business lies in its ability to focus its improvement efforts on these areas, and hence make the maximum impact on its results.

The Theory of Constraints is a method designed to identify these weak links and to determine how the weaknesses should

---

* Source material used with the authorisation of the Goldratt Institute.

be tackled. It is therefore an effective instrument for identifying short- and medium-term priority objectives, when these concern organisation and management issues rather than numerical targets. A brief description of the method is given below.

Approach

To decide on priorities for action, the first thing we must do is to identify the areas which need rapid improvement. In the engineering area, for example, it could be a question of designing a specific product or reducing new product time to market. In the administrative area the priority could be one of resolving the transfer pricing problem, defining a reliable procedure for new investment appraisal or redesigning reporting procedures in order to have an effective decision-support system. In marketing we may need to go into a new market, revise the product pricing system, or design a new commission scheme for salesmen and agents.

But for a manager the priority could simply be his or her own area of responsibility. Independently of the area chosen, we must, however, clarify one basic concept: any improvement process, be it in marketing, engineering, production or in one's personal area, must be the result of answers to the following three questions:

1 What do we change?
2 To what is it to change?
3 How do we bring about the change?

The capacity to achieve breakthroughs lies in the ability to answer these questions.

Symptoms, Causes and the Core Problem

The first step in the development of an effective improvement process is to seek out those few elements which cause the majority of the undesirable effects. The smaller the number of these elements, the more incisive, efficient and effective the improvement process will be. If we accept the fact that an undesirable effect (UDE) is usually a symptom, that is, an effect determined by a certain cause, we must agree that a search for the causes requires the analysis of cause-and-effect relationships.

We must therefore try to construct *a current reality tree,* a logic diagram which represents the way in which things work today in the area in question and which identifies the undesirable effects by identifying the links between causes and effects. Every state which does not derive from another state, that is, every entry point into the tree, must be considered to be a principal cause. It is always possible to construct a sufficiently exhaustive current reality tree for at least one entry point to include the majority of the undesirable effects. This entry point can be considered to be the main obstacle to be removed. The priority objective of all the improvement efforts should therefore be action to overcome or to neutralise it.

A typical current reality tree diagram is reproduced in Figure 5.1. An example extracted from a complete tree representing a business situation is given in Figure 5.2.

Why Has the Core Problem Not Been Resolved Already?

Everyone has intuitions and everyone wants to succeed. How then is it possible that an important problem has not already been solved? Probably there is something which has prevented a solution from being implemented. Often it is a question of internal conflicts which prevent managers from concentrating all their efforts on a a single direction (the one which can solve the problem). If this is the case, the conflict can be brought to light by the present situation analysis, through the identification of the cause of the dispersal of efforts.

To solve the main problem it is, above all, necessary to identify it and to define it clearly. Then, in order to be sure that it is the real main problem, we need to go through a phase of checking and confirmation. The process is as follows.

We express the problem identified by the current reality tree the opposite way round, i.e. in the way in which we think that

WHAT TO CHANGE?
What is the core problem?

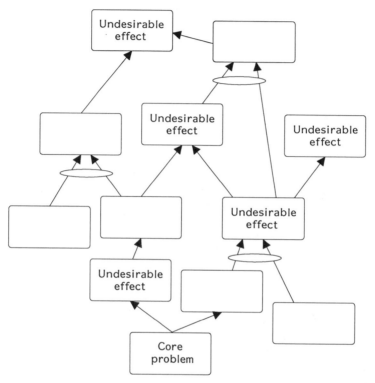

Figure 5.1 *A current reality tree—the thinking process that makes it possible to start from undesirable effects and, using knowledge already available, to pinpoint the core problem.*

all the undesirable effects disappear. This becomes the new situation to be created, the "change objective". This phase is necessary to check why it is not already that way, and where the conflict is that is preventing it from happening.

Once we have defined the problem as an "opposite" objective, we must highlight the basic conditions for achieving it, that is, the essential requirements for pursuing the objective. We then focus on identifying the conflict which emerges and on writing down the contradiction which exists between the various assumptions and which is preventing us from getting what we want (Figures 5.3 and 5.4).

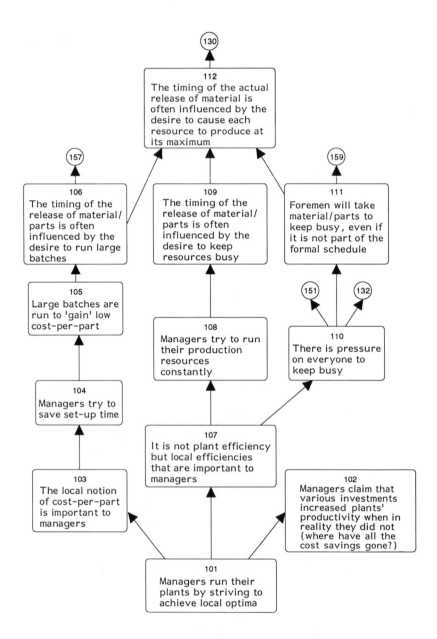

Figure 5.2 *A current reality tree: production example.*

We must avoid any attempt to compromise. If an acceptable compromise really existed, it would already have been found. The best solution is the elimination of the problem, i.e. the cause.

We must analyse what changes in the actual situation can remove at least one of the reasons of the conflict. TOC deals with this phase by constructing an *evaporating cloud*, that is, by designing the pattern of cause-and-effect relationships which will make the problem "evaporate".

The Solution to the Problem

The situation can only change if we find a breakthrough idea, that is, a change which can eliminate the conflict. The action capable of changing the situation is called an *injection* (of something new or different). But finding a possible breakthrough or

WHAT TO CHANGE TO?
Where do we look for the breakthrough idea?

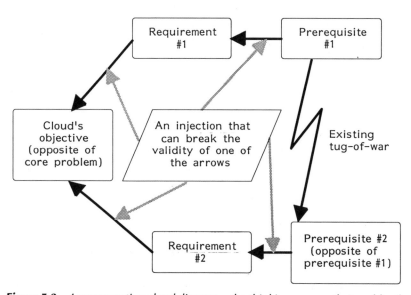

Figure 5.3 *An evaporating cloud diagram—the thinking process that enables the precise presentation of the conflict which perpetuates the core problem and directs the search for a solution through challenging the assumption underlying the conflict.*

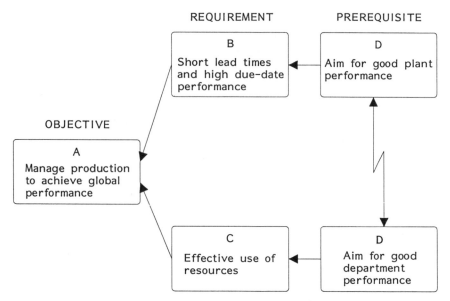

Figure 5.4   *An evaporating cloud diagram: production example.*

change idea, the "injection" that can resolve the conflict, is not the definitive step. It offers a possible point of departure, but that is not to say that the solution itself is sufficient to solve the problem.

We must not forget that the main aim is, and must remain, the elimination of the multitude of undesirable effects. The improvement efforts must produce a situation in which instead of the undesirable effects we shall find desired ones. In the light of the breakthrough idea, and relying on our knowledge of the cause-and-effect relationships, we then proceed to forecast what the future situation would be through the construction of the *future reality tree* (Figures 5.5 and 5.6).

Usually the first breakthrough idea turns out to be insufficient, but the process of constructing the future situation tree leads to the definition of the missing elements, i.e. the identification of all the breakthrough ideas necessary to obtain the desired result.

Remembering that a change can cause other problems (the side-effects of a medicine can sometimes be worse than the illness), we must now check that the solution will not provoke new undesirable effects, perhaps worse than the earlier ones. These

WHAT TO CHANGE TO?
How do we move from a breakthrough idea
(the injection) to a full solution?

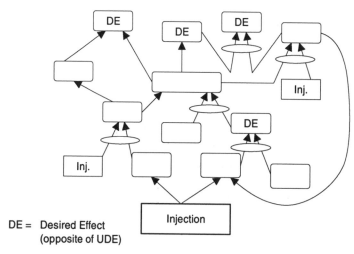

DE = Desired Effect
(opposite of UDE)

Figure 5.5 *A future reality tree—the thinking process that, through well-known links of cause and effect, enables the construction of a solution that, once implemented, replaces existing UnDesirable Effects (UDEs) with Desirable Effects (DEs) without creating new ones.*

additional efforts permit us to complete the definition of the solution, including all the elements which must be "injected" into the system in question in order to overcome the problem.

The Change Process Requires Intermediate Objectives

Once the tactical objectives of the improvement effort have been defined, we must go ahead and achieve these breakthroughs using the "injections". The future reality tree shows us how these actions will lead to the desired result and all the objectives set down.

However, implementing breakthrough ideas is not an easy task. It must not be forgotten that, by definition, at least one of the breakthrough ideas will be a break with present traditions.

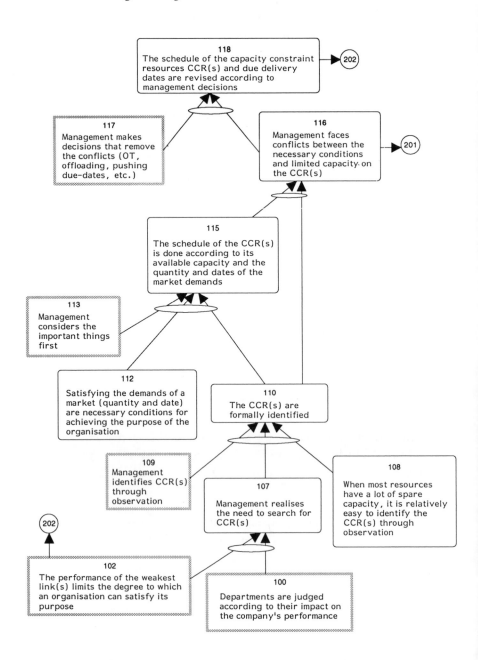

Figure 5.6   *A future reality tree: production example.*

HOW TO BRING ABOUT THE CHANGE?
Don't we have first to determine intermediate objectives?

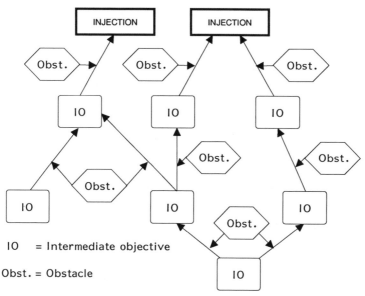

Figure 5.7   *A prerequisite tree—the thinking process that, relying on everyone's expertise to point out why something will not work (raising expected obstacles), enables division of the task on implementation into a set of interrelated, well-defined intermediate objectives.*

Because of this, it is normally necessary to divide implementation into a series of smaller steps. In order to do this, it can be useful to construct *a prerequisites tree* (Figure 5.7). By identifying the obstacles that we may encounter, we can define the specific intermediate steps which we must take, that is, the intermediate objectives or *milestones*. Each obstacle determines a milestone, an indispensable element to overcome it.

In this phase, it is important that objectives are organised in a precise sequence: what must be achieved first, which of them can be pursued in parallel, etc. The link between them comes from the fact that their interdependence in terms of time is the result of the need to overcome an obstacle. The usefulness of the *prerequisites tree* lies in the fact that it does not ignore the obstacles, but, in contrast, uses them as the main tool for identifying the implementation phases of the whole change process.

The Action Plan

Now that we have identified the main problem which is causing most of the undesirable effects, defined the direction in which to go, identified the breakthrough ideas required to achieve the desired result, set the milestones of the change process and their logical sequence, we must now go ahead and take concrete action. Without deciding on this, we cannot change the existing situation. we need an *action plan*. In deciding on the action to be taken, we must focus our attention not on what we want to do, but on what we want to achieve.

The detailed description of the change which we consider that we can progressively bring about constitutes the backbone of the

HOW DO WE BRING ABOUT THE CHANGE?
Going from here to there!

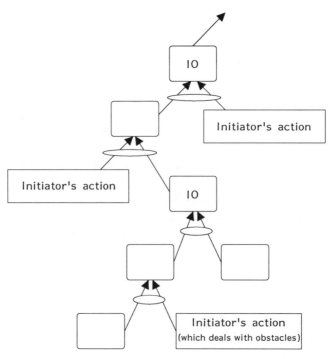

Figure 5.8 *A transition tree—the thinking process used to construct a detailed implementation plan based on the initiator's actions (the actions of others appear as restrictions). The emphasis is on the evolving change from the current situation through each of the intermediate objectives until the desired injections become reality.*

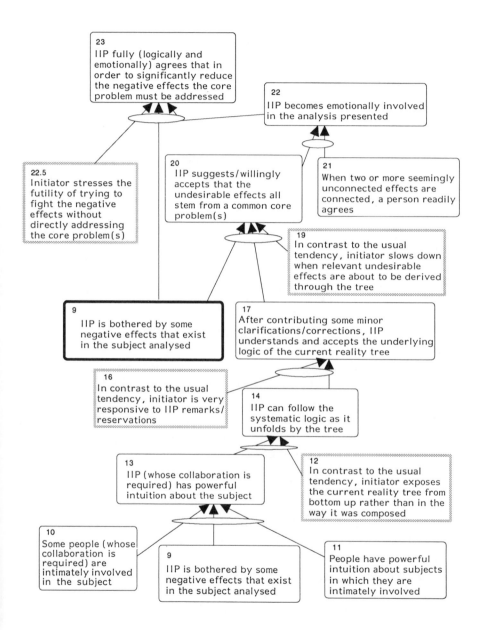

Figure 5.9   *Transition tree example: how to persuade the intimately involved person (IIP).*

change plan, the *transition tree* (Figures 5.8 and 5.9). The "ribs" attached to the backbone consist of the actions required to cause the irreversible process of gradual change to continue until the objectives have been achieved. The construction of the transition tree forces us to examine carefully which actions are really required to attack the problem, and to assess whether they will be sufficient to ensure that the desired change will occur. Too often we rely on a series of actions simply because "they are things that need to be done", without checking whether they are really adapted to the specific situation. In other words, the most important thing to do in an improvement process is to determine which are the changes necessary in reality, and not to carry out actions simply because they had already been planned. The complete logical process of the Theory of Constraints is summarised graphically in Figure 5.10.

THE AFFINITY DIAGRAM

Introduction and Description

Breakthrough management is not always dealing with clearly specified *priority objectives*. Very often it has to tackle a *priority problem* which cannot yet be defined as a clear objective. In such a case it can be useful to use an instrument designed to clarify the nature and the hierarchy of the causes of a problem: the Affinity Diagram (figure 5.11).

This is an instrument which collects a large quantity of verbal expressions (ideas, opinions, observations, etc.) coming from a number of people, and sorts them into groups having a logical and hierarchical relationship. It is one of the seven new instruments of Total Quality (N7), known in Japan as the Seven Management tools (see Chapter 4). It is a tool for managing in an effective and coherent way the integration of two approaches which traditionally are wide apart: the analytical and the creative. It is a useful instrument for organising a new activity, or for tackling a confused or particularly large, complex problem for the first time. The instrument aggregates available information into homogeneous categories on the basis of their affinity (hence its name) and then sorts it into hierarchical structures.

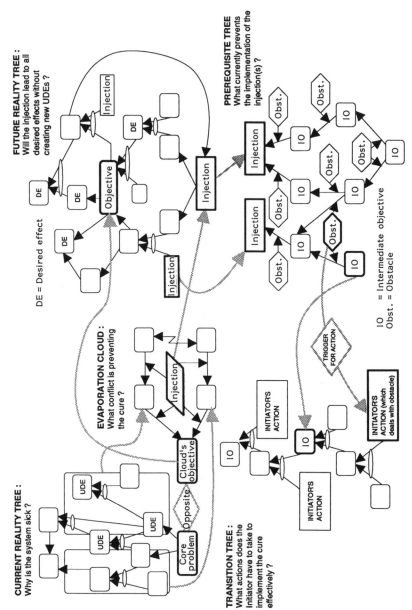

CURRENT REALITY TREE :
Why is the system sick ?

EVAPORATION CLOUD :
What conflict is preventing
the cure ?

FUTURE REALITY TREE :
Will the injection lead to all
desired effects without
creating new UDEs ?

DE = Desired effect

PREREQUISITE TREE
What currently prevents
the implementation of the
injection(s) ?

IO   = Intermediate objective
Obst. = Obstacle

TRANSITION TREE :
What actions does the
Initiator have to take to
implement the cure
effectively ?

Figure 5.10 *The TOC process.*

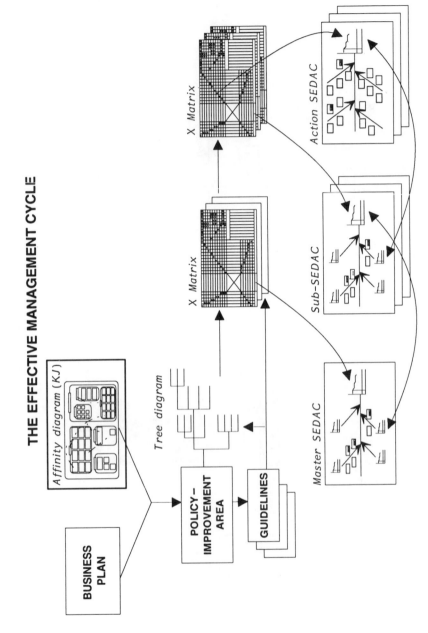

Figure 5.11 An affinity diagram as the starting point of the effective management cycle.

The Affinity Diagram was developed in the 1960s by the Japanese anthropologist Jiro Kawakita (it is also called the KJ diagram after his initials). In his work he examined the innumerable features which characterise society, organisations, movements and institutions. He made detailed notes on his observations, but when he came to analyse them he realised how laborious a task it was to find a framework to summarise such a mass of information. As a result he developed this instrument which allowed him to:

- "Sift carefully a large volume of information"
- "Express new concepts which emerge from the examination of the relationships which existed between the various pieces of information"

When to Use the Affinity Diagram

It is difficult to think of problems for which the Affinity Diagram cannot be used. But there are circumstances where its use can produce particularly interesting results. We describe below some situations in which the application of the KJ diagram has proved to be particularly useful:

- *Situations in which the information available is widely scattered and apparently does not correlate* When we examine broad, complex problems such as an organisational analysis or a marketing study, we often find a chaotic picture in which there is a great deal of fragmented information which apparently does not correlate. Under these conditions it is difficult to synthesise the large quantity of data available. In this case the use of the diagram permits us to obtain an orderly reference framework, a "map" of the problem analysed.
- *Situations in which we must overcome traditional concepts, consolidated situations, sclerotic mechanisms and solutions* When it is a question of searching for something new compared with the past, the use of the KJ method can enrich the thought processes and broaden the analysis. The Affinity Diagram does in fact help to generate new ideas and express new concepts.

- *Situations in which we must collect information from a number of people in an organised way*   The method makes it easier for a large number of people to take part in the analysis group. It makes it possible to create a large pool of knowledge to which all have contributed. The analysis is carried out with the right balance between methodical rigour, which makes for the orderly development of a process, and a very creative and detailed picture of the problem, produced by all the different angles from which it is seen by the members of the group. In particular, it guides and organises the conduct of the meetings, and makes them more effective and less dispersive.
- *Situations in which a broadly based problem must be addressed*   In some cases the elements which describe the problem range across an extremely broad, dispersed front. In these cases the method organises and structures the information available, and provides a first step towards the organisation of effective data collection.
- *Situations in which we must be sure that the analysis is complete*   The correct and complete formulation of a problem requires breadth and depth in its analysis. The Affinity Diagram facilitates this combination, helps us to construct a detailed framework and reduces the risk of going ahead without considering everything.
- *Situations in which the definition of a problem is vague and confused*   In these conditions the use of the method in the first phase to define the problem better makes it easier to organise the collection of data.

Construction of the Diagram

The identification of a problem must follow a process which especially ensures that all the aspects connected with it are understood and properly structured. Second, it must assist the in-depth examinations of its most relevant features to ensure that the problem has been fully understood. Below we give the sequence of activities necessary for the preparation and construction of the Affinity Diagram:

1   Define the problem
2   Set up the working group
3   Prepare the cards
4   Understand the cards
5   Set up the affinity groups
6   Integrate the cards
7   Look for the relationships between the affinity groups
8   Look for the most important affinity groups

Define the Problem

Formulating the purpose of the analysis is the first step in the process of developing the diagram. In the description it is better to avoid too much detail, since this could restrict the creativity of the group. Once the theme to be analysed has been classified and agreed, it is put on a board where all can see it (Figure 5.12).

Set up the Working Group

The effectiveness of the analysis made with the use of the Affinity Diagram depends on the characteristics and the composition of the team set up for this purpose. The skills and knowledge represented must be such as to cover all the facets of

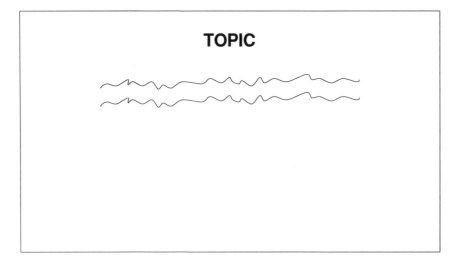

Figure 5.12 *Define the problem.*

the problem to be analysed. The team is coordinated by a leader who is responsible for conducting the analysis phase and then the synthesis of the results in a systematic manner. To assist the process of analysis it is better to keep the team down to a maximum of ten or twelve, and to have no more than two meetings of two or three hours each.

Prepare the Cards

We want to collect not only facts and data concerning the problem but also creative opinions and ideas. For this techniques such as brainstorming, observation, investigations and interviews are all useful. Elements which emerge are transcribed onto adhesive cards following the criterion "one piece of information, one card". Coloured Post-it type stickers are ideal for this purpose. As far as possible short, simple phrases should be used. All the cards should be signed so that quick follow-up is possible where classification or more details are required. The cards are stuck in any order on the board for later analysis (Figure 5.13).

Understand the Cards

The content of each card must be understood by all the members of the team. For this reason each card is read by the leader and

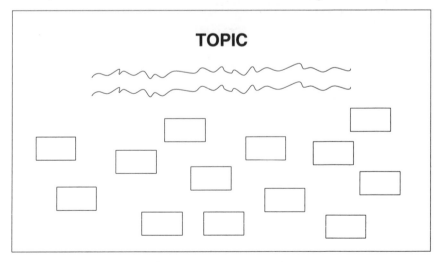

Figure 5.13   *Prepare cards.*

eventually clarified or more completely specified by the author, but without any discussion of the concept itself. It is most important that the leader handles this phase well, and avoids any discussion about its content. This would only prolong the time taken to prepare the diagram.

Set up the Affinity Groups

We now make a synthesis of the material collected. The relationships between the cards are analysed to identify any similar concepts. The cards expressing the same concept are collected together in first-level affinity groups (Figure 5.14). It is possible that some cannot be associated with any part of the framework constructed. In these cases the cards are "isolated" so as not to force them into groups to which they do not belong. Each group is given a title describing its affinity characteristic (Figure 5.15) and the title is inscribed on a different coloured card and placed above the group of cards.

For the title we must try to find a level of synthesis barely greater than the concepts expressed in its group of cards. In consequence, if in an affinity group there are more than five or six cards, it means that the titles chosen was too general. The group must be divided and new more specific titles chosen.

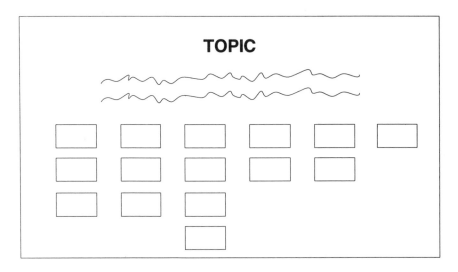

Figure 5.14   *Arrange cards into affinity groups.*

The "isolated" cards are maintained, but without titles. The process can be repeated if necessary, creating new affinities at a higher level. Starting with the titles of the first-level groups and with the isolated cards we then look for further levels of synthesis (Figure 5.16).

Finding the titles can also give the participants useful pointers for discovering further detailed issues. Normally two levels of aggregation are sufficient.

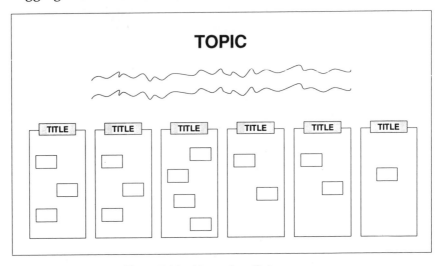

Figure 5.15 *Name the affinity groups.*

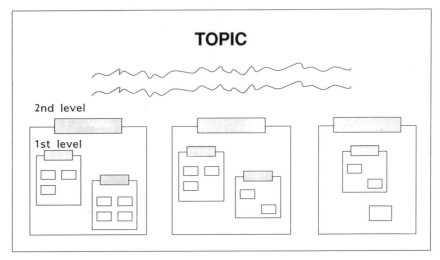

Figure 5.16 *Look for subgroups' affinity.*

Integrate the Cards

From this process of detailed analysis other aspects can come to light which were overlooked in the earlier phases, and which will further enrich the reference framework. It is therefore essential to go through a process of top-down checking in order to verify that the framework is complete, to go further into some aspects of the problem analysed, and to add new elements: "What else should be attributed to this title?".

Look for the Relationships between the Affinity Groups

Many of the elements in the framework have relationships with each other. We must therefore identify the cause-and-effect links between the affinity groups. The way to proceed is provided for in the *relationships diagram* (another of the Seven New Tools). The process is as follows:

1 Ask each member of the group which elements can be considered to be causes and which effects, and indicate the relationship between them
2 Take all the opinions into consideration
3 For the relationships on which there is general agreement, trace an arrow in the direction cause-and-effect.

Each element can originate or receive several arrows. In the case of links in both directions, it is better to draw two lines, one in each direction, rather than a single line with two arrows (Figures 5.17 and 5.18). The connecting lines representing the relationships can go from group to group, from group to card, from card to group and even from card to card.

The result depends on the theme chosen and on the construction of the diagram. At this stage it is advisable to identify only the main relationships, eventually indicating the intensity of the cause-and-effect link by the thickness of the line (Figure 5.18).

Look for the Most Important Affinity Groups

The team completes its work by identifying the most important factors on the map of the problem which it has now constructed. Suggested criteria are:

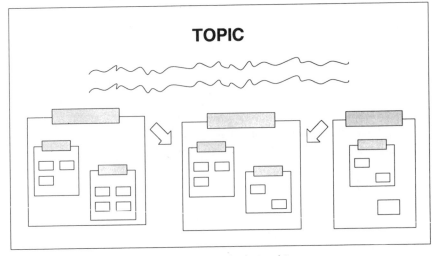

Figure 5.17   *Find relationships.*

- Assessment of the cause-and-effect relationships in terms of numbers and importance (to help in choosing the *root cause*)
- Assessment of the specific importance of each category (affinity group)

An assessment system frequently used is the award of points in order of importance (from three to one) to each of the groups. This is done individually by each member of the team. The totals determine the family which is the most important for the problem under review (Figure 5.19). In Figure 5.20 we give an example of a more sophisticated weighted example.

WINDOW ANALYSIS AND WINDOW DEVELOPMENT*

Window Analysis

Window Analysis is a technique for codifying a problem by its nature, so that we can be more effective in identifying the actions necessary to eliminate it. It can be very useful for analysing

---

* Source: Ryuji Fukuda.

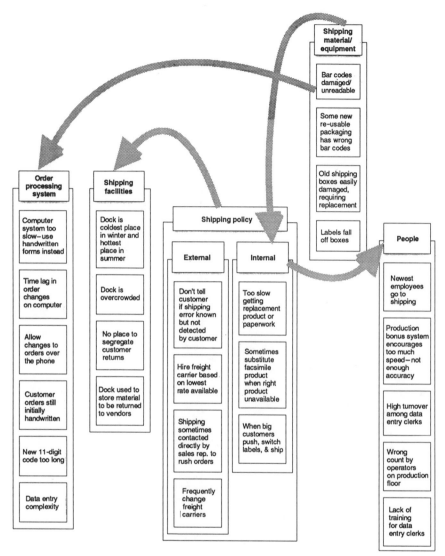

Figure 5.18   *Affinity diagram example: shipment problems.*

what type of problem is creating a bottleneck in the break-through management improvement process.

The results of this analysis will allow us to launch a suitable action programme to remove the problem, using the Windows Development methodology. The instrument consists of a double-entry matrix in which the two "units" involved in the

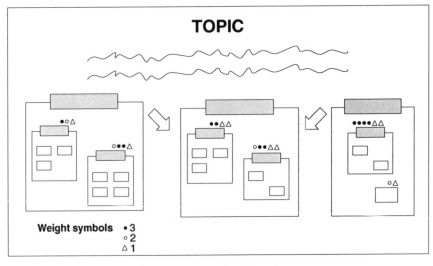

Figure 5.19   *Find relationships.*

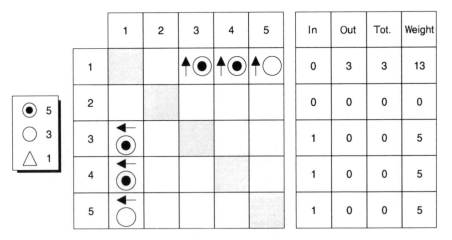

Figure 5.20   *Evaluation example.*

problem are confronted so that the best way of removing it can be found (Figure 5.21).

The steps used in Window Analysis are:

1   Definition of the problem
2   Definition of the units involved
3   Construction of the Window Analysis
4   Analysis of the results

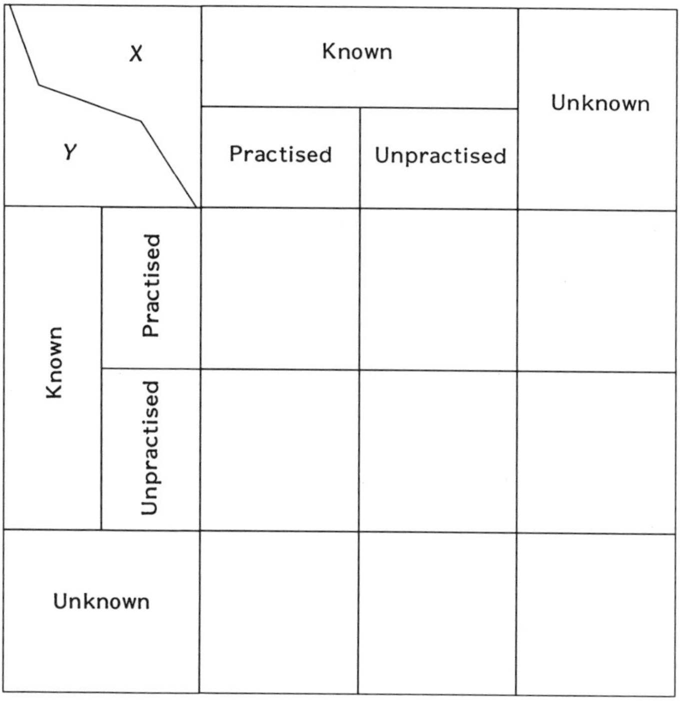

X \ Y	Known		Unknown
	Practised	Unpractised	
Known — Practised			
Known — Unpractised			
Unknown			

Figure 5.21   *Window Analysis.*

Let us see in detail how these are to be carried out.

Detailed/precise Definition of the Problem to be Analysed

The problem is described in terms of symptoms and of the negative effect to be eliminated. At this stage we must try to avoid carrying out a diagnosis of the cause.

Definition of the "Units" Involved in the Problem

By "unit" we mean a homogeneous body in terms of behaviour concerning the problem under review. The "unit" can be a function, a position, an individual, a group of persons, etc. Normally the number of units involved in a problem varies between two and four (if there are more, the problem has probably not been defined in sufficient detail).

Construction of the Window Analysis

The units confront the problem two at a time:

- Two units (XY) produce one Window Analysis (X–Y)
- Three units (XYZ) produce three Window Analyses (X–Y, X–Z, Y–Z)

The comparison must lead to each of the units choosing a "reference" situation from the three possible categories. These also show the level of knowledge of the unit involved about the method to be used to avoid the problem. The three categories (levels of knowledge) considered are:

1 *Known—Practised:* indicates that the method is known and 100% applied (completely, always, by the whole unit)
2 *Known—Not practised:* indicates that the method is known but not 100% applied (that is, not completely, always, by all the unit)
3 *Unknown:* indicates that the method for avoiding the problem is not known.

The intersection between the levels of knowledge of the two units (e.g. X and Y) determines its position among the nine possible boxes in the matrix (Figure 5.22). The nine boxes are grouped into four possible situations (A, B, C, D = combinations of the various situations of X and Y) which can be described as follows:

- *Situation A*   The method is established, known and applied by all concerned. This is the ideal situation
- *Situation B*   The correct method is established and known to all, but some do not apply it correctly or completely, or apply it only occasionally. In this category we find problems of human error, intentional negligence, lack of time, distraction
- *Situation C*   The method is correct and established, but some of the people concerned are not fully aware of it. This is due to lack of information and communication
- *Situation D*   The correct method is not established. At present no one knows it

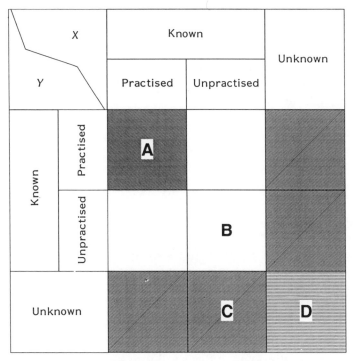

Figure 5.22 *Window Analysis categories.*

Let us look at an example of how Window Analysis is applied.

Example. The main cable of a newly designed motor for continuous use has melted after running for scarcely a week. The motor was designed by an electrical engineer and a mechanical engineer working together. The electrical engineer knew that for such intensive usage the motor needed a thicker cable, and assumed that the mechanical engineer also knew this, since it seemed obvious. In consequence, the electrical engineer did not note this in his observations on the electrical design specifications. On the other hand, the mechanical engineer knew of the relationship between the thickness of the cable required and the use of the motor, but when he was designing it, he did not apply this knowledge. Based on his design, a cable of normal thickness was installed and then burnt out through overheating.

Application of Window Analysis. Problem: burnt-out cable. X = electrical engineer, Y = mechanical engineer.

The electrical engineer (X) assumed that the mechanical engineer knew that it was necessary to use a thicker cable in the case of an electric motor designed for continuous running and did not include a note on it.

Therefore: *Known—Not practised*

The mechanical engineer (Y) did not apply his own knowledge properly when he prepared the manufacturing design.

Therefore: *Known—Not practised*

The intersection of the two situations in the window shows that the problem belongs to situation B (known by both units, but not applied by either of them).

Analysis of the Results of the Window Analysis

The results of Window Analysis fall into four categories of situation (A, B, C, D). Since the ways to solve the problem vary according to each, this diagnosis is very important. To check that the diagnosis is correct, we must not lose sight of the following:

- *Situation A*   "A" means a satisfactory situation. Such a diagnosis is theoretically impossible if there is a problem, which implies the existence of an "unsatisfactory" situation. If this should happen we need to ask the units involved to carry out another, deeper, critical analysis. We should also check whether all the units involved have been identified (the cause of the problem could lie in some "relationship" that we have not yet identified).

- *Situations B and C*   In these cases the correct method exists but it is not known completely (that is, not by everyone) or it is known by everyone but not applied by some of them (or not always). In this type of situation we must take action to understand why it is not applied, or simply explain the method correctly to everyone.

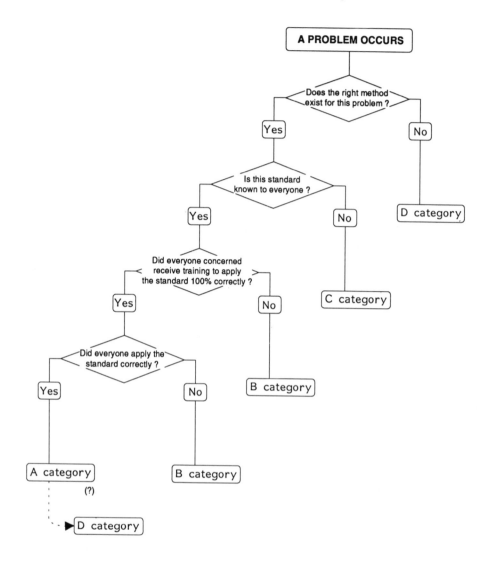

Figure 5.23 *Flow chart to analyse the cause of a problem.*

- *Situation D* In this situation there is a lack of knowledge of a "correct" method. The cause of the problem is the lack of knowledge of how to avoid it. We must therefore launch new action aimed at finding new methods (new "standards") which will eliminate or neutralise it.

In Figure 5.23 we give a decision tree which can be applied to the various situations. It is the model used by Sony as the basis for managing its operating improvement process.

Use of Window Analysis

It is not easy to apply Window Analysis immediately; it needs practice and a certain maturity in the company. At operating level there are two ways to use Window Analysis, according to the state of maturity of the firm:

1   As the first instrument to be applied in a SEDAC System environment, once the problem/obstacle to be tackled has been chosen
2   As a support to the analysis of the causes and choice of countermeasures in a project using SEDAC diagrams.

It is most frequently used in the second way.

Some Considerations Concerning Windows Analysis

Very often the Window Analysis of a problem does not result in a single pattern, but in a combination of the situation categories described (Figures 5.24 and 5.25). Let us consider the case in which the problem is the number of defects on a certain product, and various countermeasures reduce the reject rate down to a certain value (confirmed by some brief trials). Let us suppose that after a short time we carry out a more detailed check and find a reject rate higher than forecast.

In this case a more detailed analysis will probably show that some of the defects can only be reduced by redefining the standard in terms of method (situation D), while the rest are due to other causes (situations B and C). It should be pointed out that statistically a very large number of the problems found in industry are classified as category B or C.

Usually we tend to think that most of the problems arise because firms have been unable to establish the correct method (situation D). In reality, most cases (70–80%) are due to problems related to situations B and C. This means that, in general, the correct methods have been defined, but they are not known by

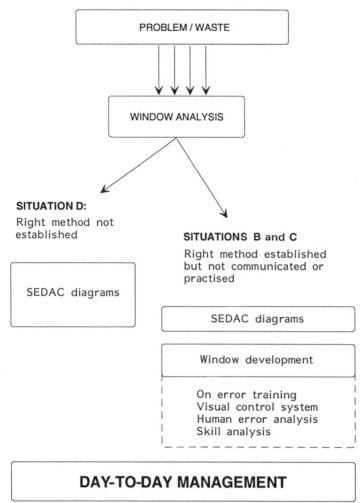

Figure 5.24 *Window Analysis activating the SEDAC process.*

everyone or they are not applied (see the data reproduced in Chapter 2).

Window Development

Window Analysis provides a classification of the causes of problems in three typical situations (zones B, C and D). To plan an improvement aiming at situation A, which must be the objective

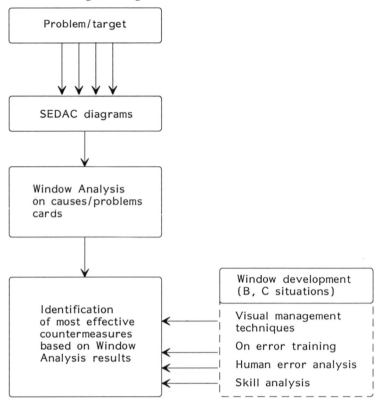

Figure 5.25   *Window Analysis and Window development in the SEDAC system.*

since it is the state which eliminates the problem, it is very important to analyse and describe the situations "not known" and "not practised" in terms of *what* is not known or not applied.

Indeed it does not necessarily mean that "not known" or "not practised" refers to all aspects of the method. It is usually a question of small details which are overlooked because they are small, but which can have very considerable negative consequences.

When the Window Analysis shows that the method is correct and defined, but not always known or practised (situations B

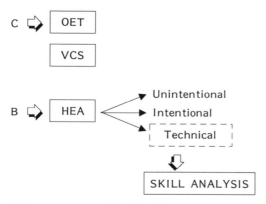

Figure 5.26 *Window development techniques.*

and C), we must "develop" the window (Window Development phase) towards situation A. For this there are a number of techniques:

- On Error Training (OET)
- Human Error Analysis (HEA)
- Skill Analysis (SA)
- Visual Control System (VCS)

A general idea of when these techniques are used is given in Figure 5.26 and a brief description is as follows.

On Error Training—OET

OET is a technique which can be used to develop a situation identified in Window Analysis when the problem is due to lack of knowledge or of application of the method. It uses the moment when the cause of the problem is visible as a means of developing the awareness and knowledge of the workers concerned, their colleagues and their boss.

It is a technique which is preferably applied to mature situations in terms of relationships between supervisors and staff, where the improvement objective is clear (that is, the search for a solution and not a culprit or a criticism of the past). OET, according to Ryuji Fukuda's original model, is based on five basic rules, three for the worker and two for the boss:

- First rule (for the worker): "himself" (it is the worker who points out the problem)
- Second rule (for the worker): "speed" (the error must be reported within half an hour)
- Third rule (for the worker): "on the job" (training must take place at the place where the error was made)
- Fourth rule (for the boss): "do not talk" (let the other talk)
- Fifth rule (for the boss): "help" (provide help)

Human Error Analysis—HEA

HEA meets another very important need: to remedy "not applied" problems (situation B), using the right improvement actions. Errors of this kind are classified by HEA into:

- Accidental errors
- Errors due to lack of capacity training, understanding of the problem and of the method (technical errors)
- Errors due to deliberate negligence (deliberate errors)

Errors made accidentally. These are due to an incapacity to maintain constant attention:

- They are not intentional
- One is unaware of making them
- They are fortuitous in time, in type of error, and so are the persons who commit them

Possible remedies are:

- Reduce the possibility of inattention
- Reduce the dependence of what is done on the need for attention (foolproofing changes)

Possible foolproofing techniques include:

- Job rotation
- Use of redundant operations (checklists of what is to be done or controlled, operations carried out twice, multiple approval, etc.)

- Use of equipment to increase the attention or focus the operation (masks, lenses)
- Introduction of equipment to attract the attention or for automatic security (alarms, shut-downs, etc.)

Technical errors. These are caused by the lack of some skill, knowledge or specific technique by the worker. Usually these errors:

- Are not intentional
- Are consolidated and repetitive
- Are specific
- Are associated with the capacity of the worker

Possible remedies are to raise the level of all the workers to that of the performance of the best worker through:

- Training
- Modifying the process technology (or the working method)
- Foolproofing

Deliberate errors. These are characterised by the fact that the worker knows perfectly well how to avoid them, but does not do so. They can be conscious or intentional errors aimed at finding a "short cut" (usually in terms of time). Possible remedies are:

- Staff motivation
- Foolproofing
- Classification of responsibilities
- Depersonalisation of orders
- Reassignment of the work

Skill Analysis

When through HEA we find a series of errors due to capacity/ training deficiencies, these can be solved by Skill Analysis. This technique offers a different, more innovative and effective way to train staff for new tasks or to acquire new skills. In Figure 5.27

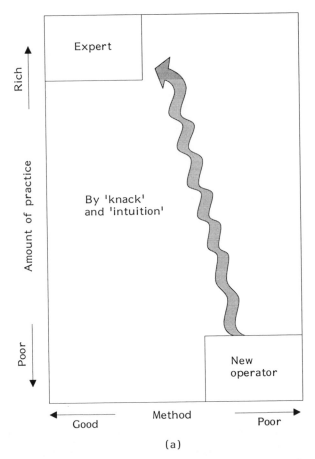

Figure 5.27　*Hypothesis on skill improvement. (a) Conventional concept; (b) (opposite) new concept.*

we make a comparison between the traditional concept and Ryuji Fukuda's new concept of training. The vertical axis represents the worker's level of experience and the horizontal axis the level of knowledge of the method. A "new" worker is located in the bottom right-hand corner.

The worker has little experience and his method is not yet very developed. But the experienced worker is in the top left-hand corner, because he has accumulated a great deal of experience and his method is sound.

The conventional approach assumes that to become capable, a long period of practice is necessary. In this situation the new

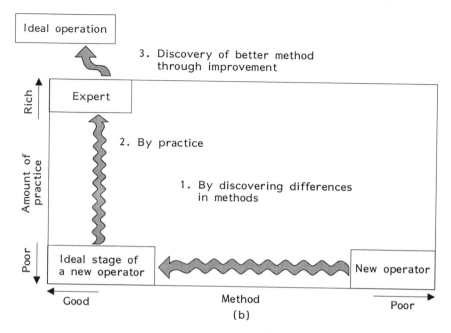

(b)

worker must count entirely on his own intuition and personal ability, repeating experiments and errors. Usually training consists of:

● Working alongside an experienced worker and "stealing his job"
● Reading manuals which contain the procedures for only the simplest operations and neglect to explain their more "delicate" features

The main assumptions of the new approach are:

1 Capacity is not synonymous with intuition and ability acquired over a long period of time
2 The main differences in capacity are due to differences of method.

In consequence, the best method known must be taught to all right from the start.

Training must therefore begin by making a comparison between the methods of the new worker and those of an experienced worker, and on an analysis of the differences. The training of the new worker will then be based on those differences. In this way the practice (experience) time required for the new worker to master the correct method is drastically reduced.

Appendix: Operating Guide— Management by Policy (Hoshin Kanri)

INTRODUCTION

Management by Policy is the management process designed to obtain breakthroughs in business performance. It can be used to improve any type of performance, from cost reduction, productivity improvement, quality improvement, through to reduction of lead time, increase of market share. It should, however, only be used on important objectives (which should themselves be part of a business plan). It is perhaps the only instrument which can successfully manage a business in a rapidly evolving environment.

Management by Policy is based on a careful, precise deployment of policies and objectives into sub-objectives and concrete actions, and on careful operating management which involves all those who are in a position to make a contribution. It is also a process for obtaining consensus over the action to the taken. The flow chart of the process is illustrated in Figure A.1.

Management by Policy has a typical time cycle of one year. For more advanced firms and the most dynamic sectors, the period can be as short as three to six months. In Figure A.2 we give the time necessary for the individual phases in the case of an annual cycle.

If the time cycle is a year and we want to launch a policy at the beginning of the year, the first phase must start in November. The budgeting process will obviously need to include a large part of the objectives and all the resources required for MBP activities. The following instructions concern the individual operating steps and assume that company policies have already been decided at top management level. It is, however, possible for the process to be used by a divisional director or an operating unit for a policy specific to itself.

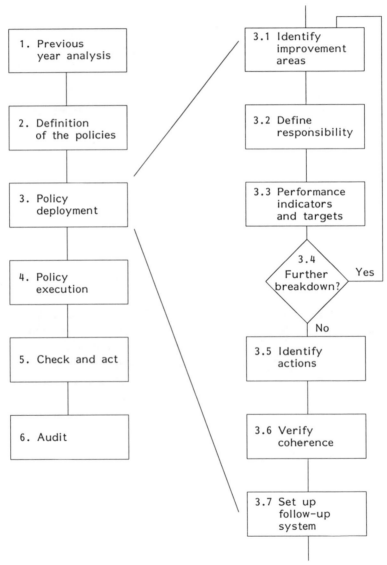

Figure A.1   *Management by policy (flow).*

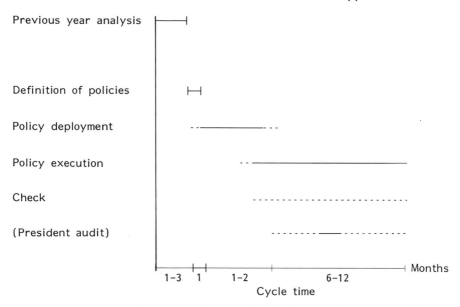

Figure A.2   *The annual cycle of MBP.*

1 THE "LOGICAL" PHASES

1(a) Analysis of the Preceding Year

Content

A full analysis is made of the problems and performance of the preceding year (or reference period). The eventual causes of the failure to meet business objectives are also identified. These are then the subject of critical analysis to identify the main problems or critical areas.

Purpose

To have a clear understanding of what are currently the main problems or critical areas of the business.

Responsibility

Top management/management board/top level operating managers. Anyone in the hierarchy can, however, be involved.

Data and Tools

Performance indicator trends, specific investigations, results of MBP audits (if already in place). Pareto Diagrams, Affinity Diagrams and eventually other more sophisticated instruments are used.

1(b) Assessment of the Scenario, Strategies, Long-term Policies

Content

Assessment of the competitive situation and identification of strategic priorities. Comparison of the priorities with the long-term policies.

Purpose

To focus on the business priorities and the policies to be considered in preparing the business plan.

Responsibility

Top management/management board, or the highest level involved.

Data and Tools

Competitive position analysis, benchmarking, strategic plan, long-term policies (from the matrix).

2 DEFINITION OF THE POLICIES AND OBJECTIVES FOR THE YEAR

Content

Policies (one to three) are defined in terms of *what and how*, based on the assessments made in phases 1(a) and 1(b).

Purpose

To define the basic priorities for which a breakthrough-type improvement is required, and "how".

Responsibility

Top management/management board/unit manager.

Tools

The following structure is recommended:

- Policy: ....
- Objective (what): ....
- Guidelines (how): ....
- Constraints: ....

See the example in Table A.1.

Note. The objective is short term, typically a year or less. The guidelines and constraints, on the other hand, must be considered over a medium/long-term timescale.

3 POLICY DEPLOYMENT

Content

In a series of steps the policies ("what" and "how") are broken down into subsidiary policies until we are able to define them in terms of actions and concrete projects. Figure A.3 gives an example.

Table A.1 Policy example.

Policy	Target	Constraints	Guidelines
Increasing of market share of "X" product	+20% by December 1991	Do not increase the number of salespeople	Priority in East European countries
		Restyling cost <3% actual product cost	Develop post-sales activities
		Same level of advertising costs	

Purpose

To set up a plan of the activities/actions required to obtain the results, involving whoever can contribute to identifying and organising them.

Responsibility

Starting with top management or the highest level involved, responsibility is then assigned to those who can and must contribute to the deployment. Top management appoints a coordinator for the development of the process, for setting the constraints for each step and for the collection of the information (the controller).

Tools

The deployment of objectives is mainly based on analysis of the data of the previous year. Use is made of instruments such as Pareto, Stratification, Cause-Effect Diagrams, Affinity Diagrams (the Theory of Constraints can also help). For each step the sub-process described below is used.

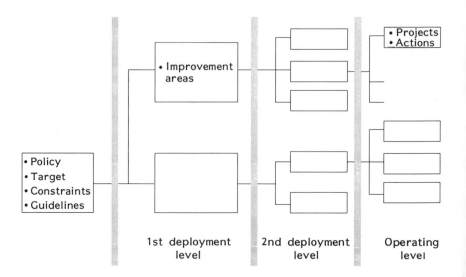

Figure A.3   *Deployment by tree diagram.*

3.1 Identification of Improvement Areas

Content

For each policy, available data are analysed to identify priority improvement areas. The best ways to sort the information must be found (by market product, sector, etc.). If the data are not available they have to be reconstructed or collected *ad hoc*.

A minimum number of priority areas on which to concentrate must be chosen at each level of deployment. Not only the figures objective but also the guidelines must be broken down. Improvement areas may be concerned with the deployment of objectives, but they may be confined to the deployment of "how".

Purpose

To identify the priority objectives on which to concentrate in order to achieve the major objective.

Responsibility

The person responsible for the objective with his or her subordinates and other people/units involved.

Tools

Data collection, Control chart, Stratification, Pareto Diagram.

Note

1   Very often deployment follows the hierarchy: the lower organisational level then becomes the improvement area. This approach is not the only alternative. Other possibilities are deployment by process or by cost element.

2   Care should be taken not to work on all improvement areas at each deployment level: priority must be given to those areas which offer the greatest contribution to the achievement of the objectives and which are the easiest/most opportune to tackle.

3   It is important to base deployment and later the quantification of sub-objectives on analysis of facts.

3.2 Definition of Responsibility

Content

For each improvement area the functions which can contribute to the required improvement must be identified. A person must also be nominated to be responsible. Usually the units which can contribute to the deployment of an improvement area are at a lower level in the organisation.

Purpose

Identify the persons or forms of organisation (individual, inter-functional study group, project group, etc.) which can organise the improvement actions required.

Responsibility

The person or group responsible for achieving the objective.

Tools

Window Analysis (SEDAC System) can be useful.

3.3 Identification of Performance Indicators and Objectives

Content

The performance indicators and the objectives for the improvement areas are usually defined at the same time as the person responsible is nominated. In many cases they can be derived directly from the data collected to identify the improvement areas (see point 3.1). In any case the objectives for the improvement areas must be checked for coherence with the main objective. At each deployment level the main objective is called the "control point", and the objectives for the improvement areas the "check points". We must remember to choose only a small number of priorities with challenging objectives at each deployment level (breakthrough approach). See Figure A.4.

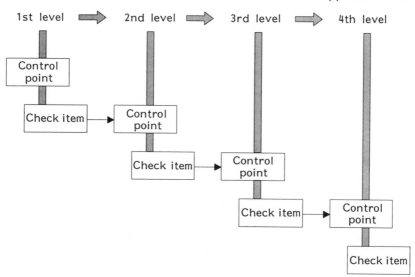

Figure A.4 *Control points and check items.*

Purpose

To define the system of management and measurement and get agreement on the amount of improvement required in the improvement areas, in order to achieve the overall objective.

Responsibility

The person responsible for the overall objective together with those responsible for the improvement areas.

Tools

The deployment can be developed through the use of *flag diagrams* bearing the performance indicators and objectives (Figure A.5). Use P/O (Policies/Objectives) Matrices to recapitulate the deployment of the objectives and to ensure their coherence (Figure A.6).

3.4 Repeat Points 3.1 and 3.3 as Necessary

Contents

The purpose of the whole deployment is to identify the concrete actions required to obtain the planned breakthrough improvement.

190

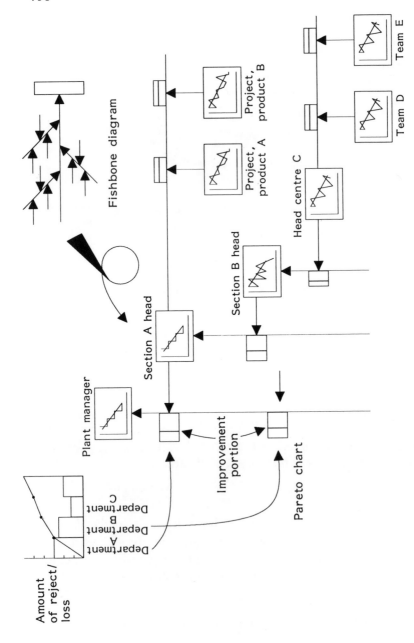

Figure A.5 Deployment in flag diagrams (Parety logic).

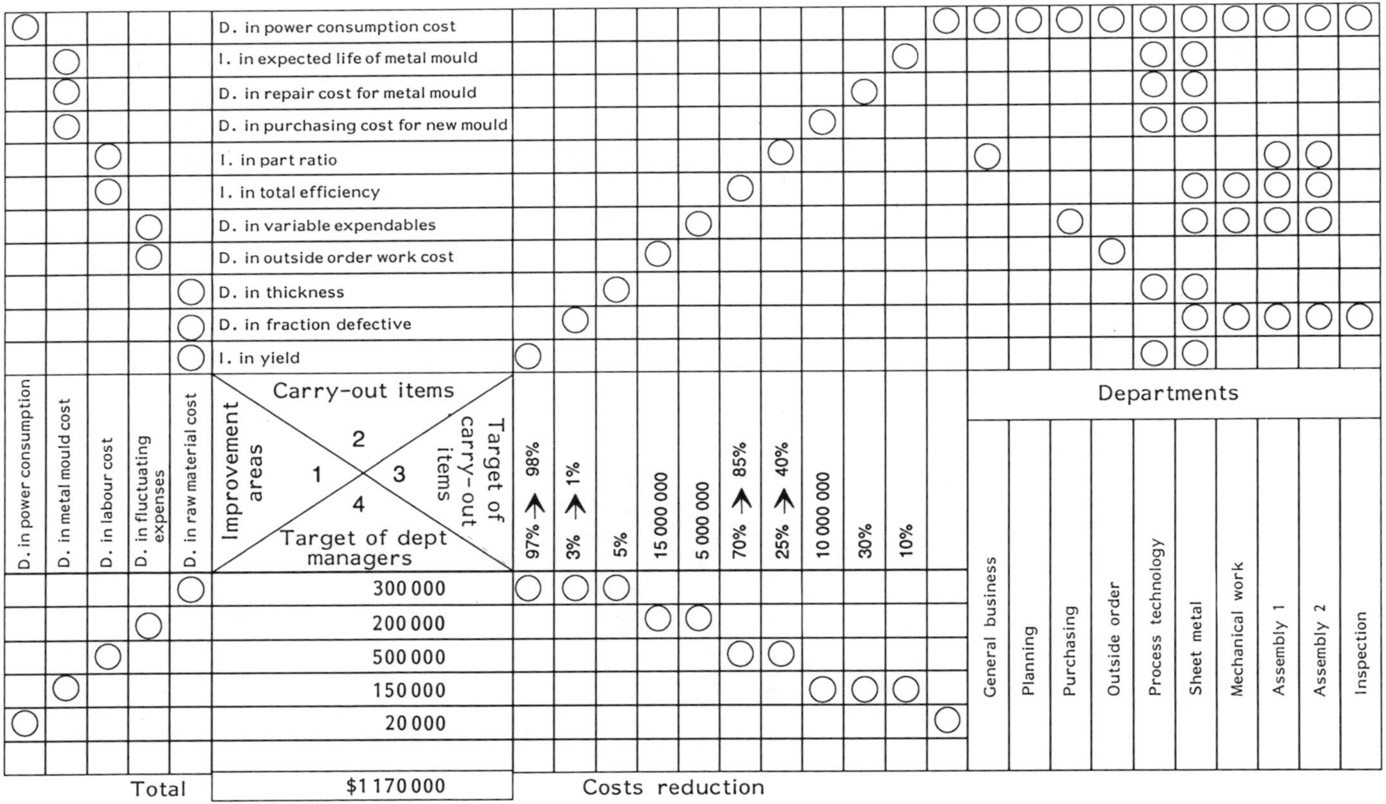

Departments

Inspection
Assembly 2
Assembly 1
Mechanical work
Sheet metal
Process technology
Outside order
Purchasing
Planning
General business

Costs reduction

10%
30%
10 000 000
25% ← 40%
70% ← 85%
5 000 000
15 000 000
5%
3% ← 1%
98% ← 97%

D. in power consumption cost
I. in expected life of metal mould
D. in repair cost for metal mould
D. in purchasing cost for new mould
I. in part ratio
I. in total efficiency
D. in variable expendables
D. in outside order work cost
D. in thickness
D. in fraction defective
I. in yield

Target of carry-out items

Carry-out items

Improvement areas

1   2   3   4

Target of dept managers

300 000
200 000
500 000
150 000
20 000

$1 170 000

D. in raw material cost
D. in fluctuating expenses
D. in labour cost
D. in metal mould cost
D. in power consumption

Total

Figure A.6   Deployment map (X Matrix).

If an improvement area is too vast (people involved, amount of data), further deployment is necessary. To do this, points 3.1 and 3.3 must be repeated until no further breakdown of objectives into sub-objectives is required. The result of the entire deployment (the operating plan) can consist of a cascade of P/O Matrices (Figure A.7).

3.5 Identification of Actions/Projects

Content

When no further deployment is required, we must proceed with the identification of the actions necessary to achieve objectives at the bottom level. Various approaches and forms of organisation are possible according to the type and size of the objective:

1   Specific individual task
2   Improvement group (often interfunctional)
3   SEDAC (with the nomination of a leader).

Many actions are not linked to any particular objective, but arise from the guidelines associated with the objectives. Various forms of organisation can be used for carrying out these actions. But each action must be programmed.

Purpose

To organise the operating improvement activities in a focused, coherent and effective way.

Responsibility

The person responsible for the improvement area, with those directly responsible for the objective/action.

Tools

Window Analysis.

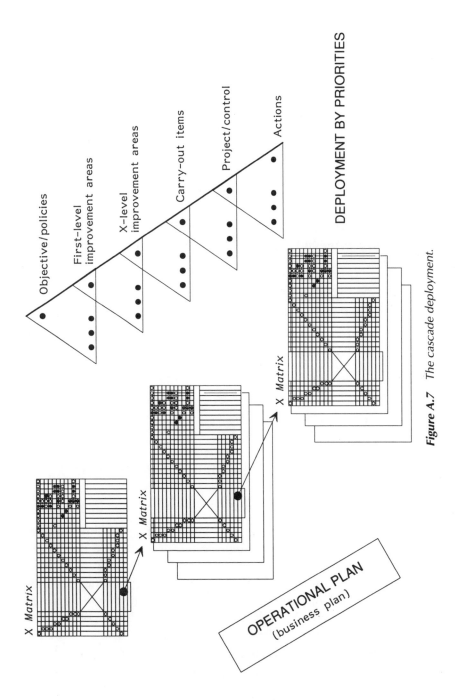

Objective/policies

First-level
improvement areas

X-level
improvement areas

Carry-out items

Project/control

Actions

DEPLOYMENT BY PRIORITIES

X Matrix

X Matrix

X Matrix

OPERATIONAL PLAN
(business plan)

Figure A.7   *The cascade deployment.*

3.6 Check the Coherence of the Deployment

Content

Once deployment has been completed, we must check if it is coherent. That is, we check whether all sub-objectives really do result in the achievement of the main objective. The P/O Matrices can be used for this. It must also be ensured that the constraints stated at the beginning have been respected and that the guidelines have been followed.

Purpose

To ensure that it is reasonably probable that the business objective will be achieved, and to eliminate possible incoherence and obstacles.

Responsibility

The person responsible for the coordination of the deployment, and all the managers involved.

Tools

P/O Matrices.

3.7 Definition of the Management System

Content

Management is based on the supervision in cascade of the performance indicators and of their coherence with the objectives. They have the task of controlling frequently (daily or at least weekly) the trends of the indicators and their coherence with the objectives (control points). They must also control the trends of the performance indicators of objectives one level below them (check points). Simple monitoring is advisable, limited to the use of graphs ("visual management"). See the examples reproduced in Figures A.8–A.10. To monitor the progress of the projects Gantt charts can also be used.

Purpose

To make effective management of the improvement activities possible.

Responsibility

The person responsible for achieving an objective is also responsible for defining the control point and check point system. He

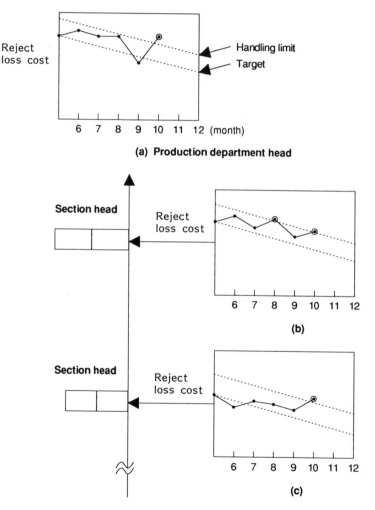

Figure A.8 The visual control.

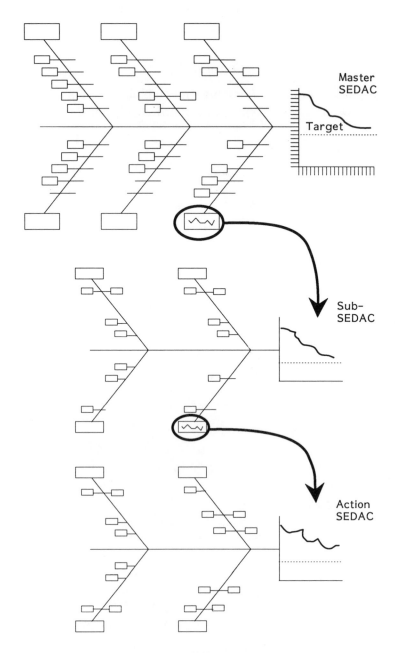

Figure A.9   *The SEDACs cascade.*

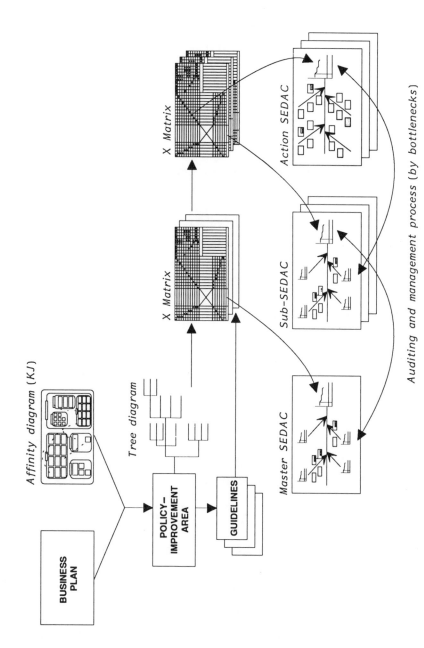

Figure A.10 Management by the SEDAC system.

or she should ensure that the monitoring system is adequate. The execution of the programme of activities should be checked by the manager of the control point.

Tools

SEDAC Diagrams, Control charts, Run charts, Gantt charts, etc.

4 POLICY EXECUTION

Content

The planned activities are activated.

Purpose

Achieve the programmed improvement.

Responsibility

All persons involved.

Tools

All those installed, plus further activities as necessary (after checking of trends by the managers responsible for the control points).

5 CHECKING AND CORRECTIVE ACTION

Content

In visual management the performance indicators must be used for a quick check. If a planned improvement is not taking place, this should be highlighted by the management system in terms of the activities which have not produced the expected result. The necessary action should then be taken as quickly as possible.

Purpose

To ensure that the desired improvement is obtained.

Responsibility

All involved.

Tools

Window Analysis.

6 TOP MANAGEMENT AUDIT

Content

In large organisations or in areas where deployment goes through several levels, an audit by top management is required. This is a formal meeting at which the managers of the various areas of the policy deployment explain how they are tackling the work. They should come from all levels in the structure. Top management must check the coherence of these programmes with company policies, ensure that the work is based on facts and not opinions, and that PDCA is being used. A simpler, more direct audit can be carried out where SEDAC instruments are being used.

Purpose

To ensure that the desired results are achieved and demonstrate top management commitment.

Responsibility

Top management must be assisted by the manager responsible for the coordination of Policy Deployment.

Tools

Window Analysis.

Bibliography

AA.VV., *Cross Functional Management*, Asian Productivity Organization, Hong Kong 1993

AKAO Y., *Hoshin Kanri*, Productivity Press, Cambridge 1991

AMES, *Market Driven Management*, Dow Jones Irwin, Homewood 1988

BLACKBURN J.D., *Time-based Competition*, Business One Irwin, Homewood 1991

COLLINS B. and E. HUGE, *Management by Policy*, Quality Press, Milwaukee 1993

D'EGIDIO F. and C. MÖLLER, *Vision & Leadership*, Franco Angeli, Milan 1992

FLORIDA R. and M. KENNEY, *The Breakthrough Illusion*, Basic Books, New York 1990

GALGANO A., *Company-Wide Quality Management*, Productivity Press, Portland 1994

GOLDRATT. E. and J. COX, *The Goal*, North River Press, New York 1994

HARRINGTON J., *The Improvement Process*, McGraw-Hill, New York 1986

HARTLEY J., *Concurrent Engineering*, Productivity Press, Cambridge 1992

IMAI M., *Kaizen—The key to Japan's competitive success*, Il Sole 24 Ore Libri, Milan, 1986

JAPAN MANAGEMENT ASSOCIATION, *The Canon Production System*, Productivity Press, Cambridge 1987

JOHANSSON H., P. McHUGH, J. PENDLEBURY and W. WHEELER, *Business Process Reengineering*, John Wiley, Chichester 1993

MAJIMA I., *The Shift to JIT*, Productivity Press, Cambridge 1992

McHUGH P., G. MERLI and W. WHEELER, *Beyond Business Process Reengineering*, John Wiley, Chichester 1994

MASKELL B., *Performance Measurement for World Class Manufacturing*, Productivity Press, Cambridge 1991

MERLI G., *Total Manufacturing Management. Production Organization for the 1990's*, Productivity Press, Cambridge 1990

MERLI G., *Total Quality Management*, Isedi, Turin 1991

MERLI G., *Comakership (The New Strategies in Purchasing)*, Productivity Press, Cambridge 1991

MERLI G., *Eurochallenge (The TQM approach to capturing global market)*, IFS, Bedford 1993

MONDEN Y., *Cost Management in the New Manufacturing Age*, Productivity Press, Cambridge 1992

NAKAJIMA S., *TPM Development Program*, Productivity Press, Cambridge 1989

PETERS T., *Liberation Management*, Macmillan, London 1992

PETERS T., *Thriving on Chaos*, Perennial Library, 1988

SANNO MANAGEMENT, Development Research Center, *Vision Management Translating into Action*, Productivity Press, Cambridge 1992

SEKINE K. and K. ARAI, *Kaizen for Quick Changeover*, Productivity Press, Cambridge 1992

SENGE P.M., *The Fifth Discipline*, Doubleday Currency, New York 1990

STALK G. and T. HOUK, *Competing against Time*, Free Press, New York 1990

WOMACK J., T. JONES and D. ROSS, *The Machine that Changed the World*, Macmillan, New York 1990

Index

Index compiled by Liz Granger